Grammatical Literacy

Grammatical Literacy

A Guide For Teachers

Susan M. Leist, EDD.
and
Melvin J. Hoffman, Ph.D.

iUniversity Press
San Jose New York Lincoln Shanghai

Grammatical Literacy
A Guide For Teachers

iUniversity Press
an imprint of iUniverse.com, Inc.

For information address:
iUniverse.com, Inc.
5220 S 16th, Ste. 200
Lincoln, NE 68512
www.iuniverse.com

ISBN: 0-595-13826-8

Printed in the United States of America

This book is dedicated to our families without whom we could not work. It is also dedicated to our students without whom there would be no reason to work.

Contents

Preface

Historical and Philosophical Backgrounds and Purpose of this Text.

The millennium bordering year 2000 more modestly marks a century's boundary too. For college language content curricula, it contrasts starkly with the prior four centuries. English grammar remains no more on the sixth through tenth grades' main menus.

Grammar entered sixteenth and seventeenth century British education to aid gentry, plutocracy, and aristocracy's sons master Latin. More representative eighteenth century student bodies studied grammar to enhance English writing and speaking skills. They learned what grammar one should use, prescriptive, rather than did use, descriptive, often learning Latin rather than English structure. The prescriptive, Latinate grammar "tradition," later depicted by Reed-Kellog[1] diagrams, survived the 19th century. Many school systems taught it into the mid-60's of the 20th century.

Some mid-60's schools used structural or generative, linguistic grammars. Traditional, Latinate, prescriptive grammar had paralleled scientific language study for 25 decades. Late 18th century scientific study started mostly in European graduate school Language, Near Eastern Studies, Philology and Comparative Literature departments. Likenesses among many European and Indo-Iranian tongues' early writings were more than accidental. Too many words with common meanings had similar pronunciations, with their differences often predictable.

Such historical-descriptive linguistic studies informed studies of early texts, philology, and inscriptions, epigraphy. Beyond confirming family affiliations, such studies altered language scholars' attitudes. For example, Latin and Greek were no longer judged ideal languages, merely Indo-European dialects that had gained standard and international status. They mirrored modern French, Italian, Portuguese, Romanian, Spanish etc, once, dialects of standard Latin, now, standards in their own right.

Standard status came not from intrinsic merit, but from political, economic or other "edges." Among related tongues, one (or more) had become a "language," and its relatives, its "dialects"; a former sister became the "mother tongue." Scholars ceased deeming dialects decaying or degenerate versions of a standard. Rather, less successful politically, dialects were thus less useful Ceconomically, and often socially—for their speakers.

Many scholars thus claimed what most others did and do reject. "No regional and/or non-standard dialect is inherently better or worse than any standard language." This does not deny that standard-language mastery economically (and often socially) benefits its speakers. For non-linguists, the latter claim's evident truth counters the former. The language that most important "successful" people discuss the most important issues in must be "better." This linguist versus non-linguist chasm has never closed.

Besides advocating dialect relativity, historical-descriptive linguists also defined a country's standard usage operationally: "national, reputable" and "current," Campbell.[2] Present day scanners, data bases and computer software make dictionary and usage-book labelings more accurate than ever before.

The early twentieth century pulled ethnology, part of anthropology, into the mix. Many ethnologists, studying speech of people whose cultures they were observing, used techniques and insights from historical-descriptive linguistics. An example was reconstructing earlier stages of vocabulary and pronunciation among related cultures of probable common origin. Usually, field-workers studied contemporary, and often unwritten, non-Indo-European languages e.g. African, Asian, Native-American and Pacific-Island languages. Such research bred American Anthropological Linguistics; European circumstances differed.

Anthropological linguists learned that people in small non-industrial societies did not speak "primitively." Rather than "limited" world views, they had equally complex "alternative" views and the ability to adapt like "civilized," "standard," and "international" languages. Such findings widened the gap between linguists and non-linguists as a relativity principle had emerged: "No language represents reality better or worse than another, merely differently."

What historical-descriptive linguists had said for dialects, anthropological linguists were saying for languages and language families. Tongues, whether termed dialects or languages, are like currency. How many people accept them, how widespread is their use, and how trusted is the authority behind them?

Structural linguists, linked both to historical and anthropological linguistics, shifted focus from past to present and from written to spoken speech. They held that current language study informed earlier language study. Like linguists before and after them, their grammatical terms and definitions reflected what language was, (descriptive) not what it should be (prescriptive.)

Universities provided linguists for liberal arts colleges, comprehensive and teacher-training institutions in Anthropology, Classics, Language, Linguistics, Literature and other departments. For the first time, Elementary and Secondary English teachers studied language scientifically. Such encounters had led some late-sixties publishers and schools to try out linguistically based language-arts texts, mostly structural. Generatively based texts arrived just about when formal grammar study had begun to be abandoned.

Meanwhile, pedagogical scholars reviewed earlier studies and compared students having and lacking formal grammar instruction. Researchers in the U.K., U.S., and elsewhere, concluded that formal grammar instruction did not improve writing. Such tests have been replicated often, with similar results. Lack of correlation between grammar study and writing progress appears independent of theoretical approach, whether traditional, structural, generative etc.

Such studies may be flawed.[3] Evaluating impact of teacher training and attitudes in the treatment group is just one concern. Still, most students did and do not like studying grammar; most teachers felt and feel the same about teaching it. Secondary Education departments; school systems; state, provincial, central and other government agencies now could justifiably jettison grammar instruction. That happened throughout the Anglophone world: Britain, Canada, the United States and elsewhere. Where grammar was taught at all, it usually adjoined another language arts activity, though usage labeling continued.

Meanwhile, between the 1950's and 1980's, authorities noted that different people used the term grammar differently. Perhaps, the most cited, Hartwell (1985)[4]—based on Francis (1954)[5]—distinguished five uses. Below are paraphrases, not citations, amplified by sources other than Hartwell.

1. The unconscious grammar whose rules we learn out of awareness as children, but which we cannot consciously access.

2. The explicit, scientific, descriptive grammar abstracted from field notes, intuition, surveys and texts.

3.   Usage or linguistic etiquette, judging a word, pronunciation or other choice as formal or informal, standard or nonstandard.

4.   Prescriptive grammar, stressing what should be, not what is, reflecting many Latin, not English, rules—for two and one half centuries.

5.   Stylistic grammar, "grammatical terms used in the interest of teaching prose style," Kolln (1981.)[6]

College writing instructors have taught students who lack formal grammar instruction for about three decades. This gap has had two obvious results.

1. Many instructors must teach basic grammar concepts and terms, a metalanguage, to discuss student writing. Discussing structural errors in student assignments requires a small common grammatical vocabulary. Now, college class time is spent teaching what once was taught in high schools.

2. Grammatical terms in dictionaries and usage guides are utterly opaque to students who have never learned them.

   To linguists, and to linguistically sophisticated non-linguists, a third disturbing effect has resulted as well.

3. School systems' and publishers' withdrawal from grammar reduced language-content in education journals and language arts curricula.

Many elementary and English education majors now matriculate without grammar or much language-content training. Yet, those who reject totally dropping grammar disagree on remedy. What, when and how to teach it is an ongoing e-discussion of the Assembly for the Teaching of English Grammar.[7] This group addresses whether or what classroom grammar's future should be.

Some areas have, at least, plurality consensus. Few advocate resumption of drill-and-kill exercises of isolated elements. Most believe that grammar should be taught in the context of real text whenever possible. Further agreement exists that what is taught should be related to writing as immediately as possible.

Specifically addressing Hartwell's fifth grammar, the authors stress vocabulary for teachers to discuss grammar with certain students. These include students who do not improve from the exposure-to-great-literature and writing-practice model alone. Such students need to be told specifically what is wrong with a consistent and persistent pattern of structural error.

Since "grammar five" instruction in this book centers on writing teaching, we regard it a rhetorical grammar. Actual texts, outside the canned examples, provide context from which to abstract grammatical forms. This book does not use meaning-based notional definitions. Instead, operationally defined definitions for parts of speech are used, requiring some memorization.

This book, a special-purpose grammar, does not exhaustively describe English structure. As mentioned before, students learn operational—not notional (meaning-based)—definitions and terms for talking about writing and speech. Traditional "grammar four" terminology is maintained because of its familiarity to those who have had any exposure to school grammar.

Redundancy in presentation of material is intentional. Past experience of the authors has indicated that any format whatever, used to present grammatical information, helps part of a class and confuses others. Therefore the same information is repeated in this grammar in different formats.

In 1998, the authors' student, Nicole Del Prince[8], concisely expressed the audience and purpose of this grammar:

We may all agree that high school students need enough grammar to use, but English majors need enough to explain.

We would like to acknowledge the invaluable help of Charles H. Leist without whose computer expertise this book would not have reached its final stage and publication.

Introduction

Dr. Melvin Hoffman and I started teaching a course called "Teaching Language" at Buffalo State College in 1997 in response to feedback from the cooperating teachers to whom our student teachers went for their practicum experiences. These cooperating teachers too often said that we were sending them student teachers that could not teach traditional grammar because they did not know it. So we created a course which combined a review of traditional grammar with study and discussion of other linguistic issues such as the right to one's own language. We soon found that the cooperating teachers had been correct —our students with few exceptions did not know the metalanguage of traditional grammar. They were unaware of the existence of subunits to the sentence. They were unable to grammatically manipulate or analyze text. Perhaps they had had instruction in grammar early in school, taught through means of canned grammar exercises, or perhaps they had had no grammar instruction. Whatever the case, they did not know traditional grammar and could not analyze real text.

We started using popular writer's references as recommended textbooks, but we soon found them to be inadequate because of the peculiar organization each had for its section on grammar. Sometimes they began with a section called "Parts of Speech"; sometimes they ended with one. Always, though, this section had no connection to the rest, and the rest was a confusion of information about clauses, phrases, functions, labels, and exceptional usages. Our students and we could look things up in them-if we already knew what we needed to find. For those who did not have the metalanguage AND some grasp of the whole corpus of traditional grammar, these references proved pretty much useless.

This textbook, then, is our compilation of materials we have created for the course. We start our review with the Sentence as a basic unit and begin immediately to explore the subunits incorporated in sentences. As that exploration proceeds, using always real text rather than tailored exercises, we have to find out about the various functions of subunits. We use the parts of speech as a category system for form and function, gathering together all the information about each part of speech, how it can function and how groups can function in its capacity. A continuous strand is the emphasis on form and function.

Our aim for the grammar component of this course is to teach the metalanguage of grammar and enable our students to both perceive and use it as a means to explore the terrain of real text. We emphasize the fact that "correctness" in writing is a side issue in this study, letting students build a set of copyediting symbols as they see grammatical issues bleeding over into composition issues. For example, they begin to see "faulty parallelism" as a composition error after they can separate sentences units that should carry parallel construction. They only really understand "dangling" or "misplaced" modifiers after they can perceive subordinate clauses or infinitive phrases as modifiers.

Generally, the process can be done in a semester. Soon our students have the metalanguage, and they can grammatically analyze real writing. We hope that our reorganization of traditional grammar components proves as useful in your teaching as it has in ours.

—Susan M. Leist
June 10, 2000

Chapter I

SENTENCES

A. Predicate:

1. must contain at least one Main **Verb** (the rightmost in a Verb Group) which may be modified by other words and

2. must have one of the following three Predicate Markers (the leftmost in a Verb Group.)

   A. The verb itself in past form or in present form agreeing with the subject role.
   B. The helping/auxiliary verbs do/does/did, have/has/had, or am/is/are/was/were in the past form or in the present form agreeing with the subject.
   C. The helping/auxiliary verbs can/could, will/would, shall/should, may/might, or must. (This group of helping verbs are sometimes called Modals.)

Every predicate includes a verb or verb group, but not every verb or verb group is a predicate.

subject + predicate
(Sentence)

subject—no predicate
(Fragment)

Markers are italicized and Main Verbs are underlined.

John + *sees*/*saw* him.
[Present/Past Tensed Verb leftmost AND rightmost Both Marker and Main Verb]

John—seeing/seen him.
[No Past or Present Tense—No Marker, only Main Verb]

Mary + *has*/*had* done it.
[Present/Past Tensed Helping Verb, Leftmost, Marker, followed by Main Verb, Rightmost]

Mary—having done it
[No Past or Present Tense—No Marker, only Main Verb]

I + *am*/*was* understood.
[Present/Past Tensed Helping Verb, Leftmost, Marker, followed by Main Verb, Rightmost]

I—being/been understood
[No Past or Present Tense—No Marker, only Main Verb]

They + *have*/*had* been helped.
[Present/Past Tensed Helping Verb, Leftmost, Marker, followed by Main Verb, Rightmost]

They—having been helped
[No Past or Present Tense No Marker, only Main Verb]

We + *could* have <u>helped</u>.   xxxxxxxxxxxxxxxxxxxxxxxx
[Modal Helping verb, Leftmost,

Marker, followed by Main Verb,
Rightmost]

A Subject:

must be a noun, pronoun or group of words that can take a personal
pronoun as a substitute.

<u>It</u>	+ is important.	All the subjects
<u>The idea</u>	+ is important.	in the list of
<u>To work</u>	+ is important.	examples on the
<u>What he did</u>	+ is important.	left could take
		the pronoun 'it'
		as a substitute.

<u>The man whom I met</u>	+ is happy.	'he'
<u>The waitress in the restaurant</u>	+ was efficient.	'she'
<u>The people working in the plant</u>	+ received a raise.	'they'
<u>My friend and I</u>	+ walked home.	'we'

A Sentence is a group of words which has a Subject and a Predicate.
(This statement will be slightly amended later.)

WAYS OF CLASSIFYING SENTENCES

1. BY CLAUSE:

Simple—S-V

She has a summer cold.
A good man nowadays is hard to find.
The autumn leaves fall gently to the ground.
A class next door clapped loudly.
He was a tall, lanky fellow.

Compound—S-V (; or , conj) S-V

She has a summer cold, and her nose runs constantly.
A good man nowadays is hard to find, but bad ones are thick on the ground.
The autumn leaves fall gently to the ground, and the trees are bare in winter.

A class next door clapped loudly, but their teacher made them stop.
He was a tall, lanky fellow, but his wife was very small.

Complex—1. Subordinating conjunction S-V,
S-V or S-V subordinating
Conjunction S-V

When she has a summer cold, her nose runs constantly.
Though a good man nowadays is hard to find, bad ones are thick on the ground.
After the autumn leaves fall gently to the ground, the trees are bare all winter.
Because a class next door clapped loudly, their teacher made them stop.
He was a tall, lanky fellow while his wife was very small.

2. S-V with (relative pronoun or adverb S-V) inside.
Clauses beginning with relative pronouns or relative adverbs *{who/whose/whom, what which; when, where, why, how}* can act as nouns, adjectives, or adverbs. If nouns, the word starting them does NOT have an antecedent in the sentence. If adjec-tives, the word starting them HAS an antecedent in the sentence.

She has a summer cold which makes her nose run.
A good man nowadays is hard to find when bad ones are thick on the ground.

*The trees are bare all winter when the autumn
leaves fall gently to the ground.*
*A class next door, whose teacher made them
stop, had clapped loudly.*
*He was a tall, lanky fellow whose wife was very
small.*

Compound complex-1.Sub. Conj. S-V, S-V (conj. or ;)
S-V. [Or any combination thereof]

*Since she has a summer cold, her nose runs con-
stantly, and she uses boxes of tissues.*
*Though a good man nowadays is hard to find,
bad ones are thick on the ground, so hang on to
the one you have.*
*After the autumn leaves fall gently to the ground,
the trees are bare all winter, and the snow lies
thickly on the ground.*
*Since a class next door clapped too loudly, their
teacher made them stop, but she could not keep
them from laughing.*
*Though he was a tall lanky fellow, his wife was
very small, and his children were average sized.*

2. S-V (, conj. or) S-V with (relative pronoun S-V) inside. [Or any combination
thereof.]

*She has a summer cold which makes her nose
run constantly, and she uses boxes of tissues.*

*A good man nowadays is hard to find when bad
ones are thick on the ground, so hang on to the
one you have.*

*The trees are bare all winter when the autumn
leaves fall gently to the ground, and the snow
lies thickly under them.*

*A class next door, whose teacher made them
stop, had clapped loudly, but now they are
laughing.*

*He was a tall, lanky fellow whose wife was very
small, and so their children are all average sized.*

Sentences can be classified in various ways, and they can be combined in various ways. When sentences are discussed in terms of classifications and/ or combinations, they are called *clauses.*

Certain word groups need to be memorized before sentences can be classified.

The first group, seven words, is called **coordinating conjunctions.** Some of these words do more than one job, but we are concerned here just with their sentence connecting roles:

And, or, but; for, yet, so; nor.

The second group, fifteen words, is called **subordinating conjunctions.** Some of these words do more than one job, but we are concerned here just with their sentence introducing roles. One is listed twice.

(al)though, because, if, since(1), that, unless, until, whether, while; after, before, since(2), once; as, like (informal), than.

[Some grammars use the terms Dependent and Subordinate Clause fairly synonymously. This grammar will distinguish the terms.]

Dependent Clauses may be headed by two other sets of words other than Subordinate Conjunctions. These two sets are called Relative Adverbs and Relative Pronouns.

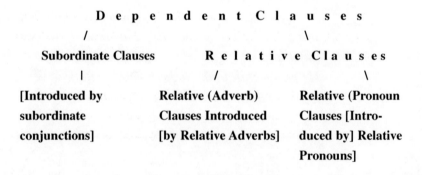

	D e p e n d e n t C l a u s e s	
/		\
Subordinate Clauses	**R e l a t i v e C l a u s es**	
		/	\
[Introduced by subordinate conjunctions]	**Relative (Adverb) Clauses Introduced [by Relative Adverbs]**	**Relative (Pronoun Clauses [Introduced by] Relative Pronouns]**

In "contemporary" traditional grammars, Subordinate & Dependent Clauses are often synonymous, and Relative Adverbs may lump with "Subordinators/Subordinating Conjunctions." Sometimes, even the Relative Pronouns may lump with them, but not as often. However, even "lumping " textbooks may separate either or both relatives in discussion, so they are treated here separately from each other and from Subordinating Conjunctions.

Relative pronouns: who/whose/whom, which, what, that

Relative adverbs: how, when, where, why, that

All these words may function as interrogatives (question words) in question-word questions like "Who are you?" and "How is it?" with the exception of the "that's."

All but the "that's" may take the extender "-ever": whichever, whatever, whoever/ whoever/whomever, however, whenever, whyever*. (Not all of them occur in every English dialect however. Asterisks mark forms with regional distributions.)

All the relative pronouns except the "that's" (and—in some dialects, some of the relative adverbs—particularly "how") take the extender "soever": whosoever/ whosesoever*/ whomsoever, whichsoever*, whatsoever, howsoever.

"Which" and "What" have exclusive distributions. "What" always introduces a clause for which "it" may substitute:

[What he did] is right.   [It] is right.
I know [what it was.]   I know [it.]

"Which" introduces clauses that modify some noun to the left:

the car which I drove,   the machine which ran well etc.
    <————| <———————-|

The Disappearing Relatives and Subordinate Conjunctions (Subordinators)—Zero Form.

Relative Pronouns when direct objects (and in special cases) as well as Relative Adverbs (in special cases) may take "that" as a substitute or disappear altogether:

the man whom	I met,	the car which	I drove,
the man that	I met,	the car that	I drove,
the man Ø	I met,	the car Ø	I drove,
the place where	I was,	the day when	I left,
the place that	I was,	the day that	I left,
the place Ø	I was,	the day Ø	I left,

the reason	why	I went,
the reason	that	I went,
the reason	Ø	I went,

The Subordinate Conjunction that may also disappear under certain conditions:

I see that it is true.
I see Ø it is true.
I have an idea that it is true
I have an idea Ø it is true.

It is important that it is/be true
It is important Ø it is/be true.

Sometimes clauses with "disappearing" introducers are hard to recognize as dependent clauses. Be careful.

Each clause has a SUBJECT and a PREDICATE.

A Dependent   with a RELATIVE PRONOUN, RELATIVE AD-

Clause begins   VERB OR SUBORDINATE CONJUNCTION.

An Independent Clause does not begin with one of those.

WAYS OF CLASSIFYING SENTENCES

2. BY COMPLEMENT:

      Intransitive

      Subject complement adjective

      Subject complement noun

Direct object

Indirect object

Object complement noun

Object complement adjective

The second way to type sentences is to identify the complement of the sentence. Checklist of Guidelines determining whether a noun or pronoun complements a verb.

A noun/pronoun complements a verb, providing all four of the following provisions are met.

I.   Both the verb and noun/pronoun which are in a verb and complement relationship must be headwords. That is, Words can modify them, but they cannot modify other words.

Correct Pair   Incorrect Pair

I heard the bell.   *I climbed the bell tower.*

Time is money.   *She is flying the plane.*

           me   *me*
He gave a choice.   *He gave a choice steak.*

           him   *him*

She did a favor.   *She did call a gentleman.*

The men had a bargain.   *The men had lost their bargain.*

II.   Both the verb and noun/pronoun which are in a verb
and complement relation cannot have a preposition and/or
different verb headword in between them.

      Correct Pair   Incorrect Pair

      We waited an hour.   *We waited for him*
                                         ^

      They sang a tune   *They wanted to sing a tune.*
                                    ^ ^

      She kept the work.   *She kept doing the work.*
                                     ^

      The people saw it.   *The people saw to it.*
                                       ^

      You helped the students.   *You helped teach the students.*
                                   ^

III.   No Relative Pronoun or Adverb, or Subordinate
Conjunction, present or implied can occur between
the verb and noun/pronoun headwords.

      Correct Pair   Incorrect Pair

      He played the game.   *He played after the game ended*
                                     ^

      Joe won prizes.   *Joe won what prizes they had.*
                                     ^

      Mary left the party.   *Mary left when the party ended.*
                                     ^

I knew something.   *I knew if something happened.*
                                                    ^

They felt it.   *They felt (that) it was true.*
                                                    ^

VI.   "Normal" word order (subject verb [complement]) is always
         assumed in the instruction: "Noun or Pronoun Headword after
         a Verb Headword."

         "Hello, said John   = John said, "hello."
         "Caesar, Brutus stabbed." = Brutus stabbed Caesar

   The words "modifier" and "modification" are used frequently in this
grammar. Below is a "rule of thumb," not absolutely tech-nical defini-
tion: "A modification pair is composed of two words: a modifier and a
headword. The modifier narrows possibilities; the headword expands
them," e.g.:

                                                    people

tall *people*   **very** *tall*   *tall* —->
—->   —->   m   h
m   h   m   h

                                                 very —->
                                                  m   h

Sentence Types by Complements

Parts of Speech and Word Groups which can Be Complements

1.   Adjectival Complements:

      A.   Adjective Complement
      B.   Adjective Phrase Complement

2.   Nominal Complements:

      A.   Pronoun Complement,
      B.   Noun Complement,
      C.   Noun Phrase Complement,

3.   Word Groups that can take a Pronoun Sub-
      stitute and also act as Nominal Complements

      A.   Verb Phrase
      B.   Infinitive
      C.   Subordinate or
            Relative Clause

(Note these same word groups have other functions when they DO NOT take a pronoun substitute.)

More about Complements: There can be none, one or two complements of a verb.

Figure I.

No Complement

(There)	If the predicate has none of the
|	above complements and is preceded
_|_ .	by "there," the sentence is
|	an expletive sentence.

There <u>is</u> a book* on the table.   The nouns marked by the asterisks* are
There <u>appears</u> to be a problem.   not predicate nomi-natives but are sub-
There <u>seems</u> no answer* to it.   jects out of normal word order, e.g # 1.
There <u>arose</u> such a clatter*.   in normal order is "A book is on the
There <u>might be</u> a chance* to win.   table."

|	If not preceded by "there," a
_|_ .	sentence without noun or ad-
|	jective complements is an
	intransitive sentence.

They <u>worked</u> with great energy.

She <u>moved</u> there yesterday

We <u>agreed</u>.

He <u>talked</u> out of turn.

The passengers <u>flew</u> home.

One Complement: **(Adjectival) or (Nominal)**

                    Referring Back to Subject

                    Because of their similarities, some people call *both* the adjective *and* the nominative complement sentences below: *subject complement* sentences.

                    If the adjectival complement refers back to the subject and follows a linking verb, the sentence complement type is a *predicate adjective*;

This <u>looks</u> <u>good</u>.

Their dinner <u>was</u> <u>excellent</u>.

The weather <u>turned</u> <u>cold</u>.

Our car <u>became</u> <u>warm</u> from the sunlight.

The visitor <u>kept</u> <u>quiet</u>.

                    If the nominal complement refers back to the subject and follows a linking verb, the sentence complement type is a *predicate nominative*.

They <u>were</u> <u>the winners</u>.

The player <u>became</u> <u>the team captain</u>.

Our dog <u>looked</u> <u>a sight</u> after his bath.

The woman <u>seemed</u> <u>a natural</u> at the sport.

She <u>played</u> <u>the lead role</u> in the film.

One Complement: **(Nominal) Different from Subject**

|
| .
|

If the nominal does not refer back to the subject and follows a non-linking verb, the sentence complement type is a *direct object*.

The people <u>had</u> <u>an interest</u> in the work.

They <u>kept</u> <u>a lid</u> on it.

She <u>had</u> <u>a new job</u>.

We <u>read</u> <u>the menu</u>.

You <u>saw</u> <u>their attitude</u>.

Two Complements:

```
| | \
| | \ .
|
```

(Adjectival) or (Nominal) 2nd. Complement Referring Back to 1st. Complement.
If the 2nd. complement is an adjectival and refers back to the 1st nominal complement, the sentence complement type is an *object complement adjective*.

They <u>made</u> <u>him</u> <u>mad</u>.

He <u>took</u> <u>it</u> <u>easy</u>.

She <u>kept</u> <u>them</u> <u>quiet</u>.

The man <u>wore</u> <u>his hair</u> <u>long</u>.

We never <u>had</u> <u>it</u> <u>so good</u>.

```
| | \
| | \ .
|
```

If the 2nd. complement is a nominal and refers back to the 1st. nominal complement, the sentence complement type is *object complement nominative*.

Voters <u>elected</u> <u>her</u> <u>governor</u>.

They <u>judged</u> <u>him</u> <u>the winner</u>.

The patrol board <u>kept</u> <u>them</u> <u>prisoners</u>.

Colleagues <u>named</u> <u>you</u> <u>woman of the year</u>.

People <u>called</u> <u>us</u> <u>close friends</u>.

Two Complements: (Nominal) 2nd. Nominal Complement not referring back to 1st. Complement.

If the 2nd complement does not refer back to the first complement, the sentence complement type is an *indirect object*.

We *showed them the door*.

She *gave him a chance*.

I *lent you a pen*.

He *asked us a question*.

Someone *sent his friend a message*.

3. BY RHETORICAL PURPOSE:

Declarative (Statements)

Interrogative (Questions)

Imperative (Requests, Commands)

Exclamatory (Expressions of intense emotions
which are often introduced by
INTERJECTIONS.
oh, gosh, well, wow.)

(Rhetorical purpose is a category system that depends on interpretation
of meaning and has, therefore, a punctuation component)

Chapter II

PARTS OF SPEECH

In as many instances as possible throughout this section, initial examples are taken from the speech by Patrick Henry titled <u>Give Me Liberty or Give Me Death.</u> At the beginning of the first appendix, Dr. Hoffman has performed an extensive grammatical analysis of that speech which yielded these examples.

WHAT NOUNS CAN DO:

All the Things That *Nouns* Can Do:

1. **Subject**—the central actor in a sentence; may be *simple, complete or compound*

SUBJECT (Sb)

These^{Sb} are the implements^{PN} of war^{OP} and subjugation;^{OP} the last arguments^{PN} to which kings^{Sb} resort.

—P. Henry

The news is exciting.
If they agree, you have a majority.
Give it a rest, and we will try again tomorrow.
The new men and the new women will replace those who retire.
I saw him after the party ended.

2. **Direct Object**—the recipient of the action of the verb in a S-V set

DIRECT OBJECT[Different Reference than Subject] (DO):

Trust it^{DO} not, sir;^{DA} it^{Sb} will prove a snare to your feet.^{OP} Suffer not yourselves^{DO} to be betrayed with a kiss.^{OP}

—P. Henry

Hit the road.
Walk softly and carry a big stick.
I thought I saw a pussycat.
They had a ball.
After we watched the game, we ate dinner nearby.

3. **Subject complement/nominative**—completes the subject by renaming it equally on the right side of a linking verb.

SUBJECT COMPLEMENT Nominative [Same Reference as Subject] (SCN):

These^Sb are the implements^PN of war^OP and subjugation;^OP the last arguments^SCN to which kings^Sb resort.

—P. Henry

She was the winner.
It became a nuisance.
He looked the picture of health

The food tasted the same as before.
They stayed members of the club.

4. **Indirect object**—recipient of the indirect or secondary action of the verb in a S-V set

INDIRECT OBJECT [Complements with Different Referents] (IO):

Give me a break.
The prosecutor promised the defendant a reduced sentence.
We made our customers a better product.
The host asked the contestants hard questions.
The judge awarded the winning entry a blue ribbon.

5. **Appositive**—completes the subject by renaming it adjacent to the subject

NOUN IN APPOSITION (Ap):
John, <u>my old roommate</u>, came to visit.
<u>A major contest</u>, the game played to a full arena. (Front Modifier)
My motion, <u>one of several</u>, was tabled until the next meeting.
Her Honor <u>the mayor</u> toured her community. (No Pauses Needed)
The patient, <u>a highly motivated person</u>, persisted in his therapy.

6. **Objects of prepositions**— "down the street…"

OBJECT OF A PREPOSITION (OP):

Our petitions[Sb] have been slighted; our remonstrances[Sb] have produced additional violence[DO] and insult;[DO] our supplications[Sb] have been disregarded; and we[Sb] have been spurned, with contempt,[OP] from the foot[OP] of the throne![OP]

—P. Henry

I'll be there, in <u>a minute</u>.
They ran out (of) <u>the door</u>.
To the <u>victor</u> belong the spoils.
Think nothing of <u>it</u>.
He wouldn't put it near <u>the house</u>.

7. **Adverbs (Adverbial object)**—nouns used as adverbs. "Joe went home." "I did it my way." "I saw him this morning."

ADVERBIAL OBJECT/NOUN USED AS ADVERB (AO):

She saw him <u>this morning</u>. (when)
They all went <u>home</u>. (where)
I did it <u>my way</u>. (how)
<u>Next year,</u> We will see you. (when)
He flew <u>first class</u>. (how)

8. **Adjectives (Noun adjunct)**—nouns used as adjectives.

NOUN ADJUNCT: NOUN USED AS AN ADJECTIVE (NA):

She is a <u>camp</u> counselor.
I saw him <u>Sunday</u> morning.
We ran from the <u>storm</u> system.
They got on an <u>entrance</u> ramp.
He found the <u>stone</u> bench.
a <u>hood</u> ornament
a <u>truck</u> garden
a <u>garden</u> pest

9. **Direct address (Vocative)**—names, pronouns, or titles

VOCATIVE/NOUN IN DIRECT ADDRESS (DA):

Sir,DA weSb have done everythingDO that could be done to avert the stormDO which is now coming on. Trust it̲DO not, sir;DA itSb will prove a snare to your feet.OP

—P. Henry

Anybody̲, is anyone here?
You̲, get over here now.
John̲, would you come over here for a minute?

Miss Jones̲, may I congratulate you on your promotion.
May I help you, Madame̲?

10. **Object complement/nominative**—renames a direct object after a transitive verb.

OBJECT COMPLEMENT [Complements with Same Referents(OCN):

The governor appointed an old friend his budget director.
The teacher made the topic the subject of discussion.
We elected her chair of the committee.
The team named John their captain.
She considered him a friend.
They call a spade an agricultural implement.

11. Objects or complements of gerunds.

teaching functional grammar

being a leader

12. Objects or complements of infinitives—

It is in vain, sir, to extenuate the matter.

—P. Henry

to teach functional grammar

to be a leader

Word Groups that function as nouns:

ANY GROUP OF WORDS—WHICH CAN TAKE A PRONOUN AS A SUB-
STITUTE—IS USED AS A NOUN: (NOMINAL)

Figure II.

<u>To   Err </u> is human.   Form: Infinitive
it/this/that   Function: Noun

I know <u>what she did. </u>   Form: Relative Pron. Clause
    it/this/that   Function: Noun

<u>Doing your best</u> is important.   Form: Pres. Part. Phrase
it/this/that   Function: Noun

<u>The man in church</u> was quiet.   Form: Noun Phrase
He   Function: Noun

They saw <u>my brother and me. </u>   Form: Noun Phrase
    us   Function: Noun

<u>Whether it works</u> is doubtful.   Form: Subordinate Clause
it/this/that   Function: Noun

<u>When he did it</u> was yesterday.   Form: Relative Adv. Clause
it/this/that   Function: Noun

WHAT PRONOUNS CAN DO:

1. Take the place of a noun in any role. (Noun replaced is called the *antecedent.*)

    John.....he   *Sarah......she*

2. Be in different *cases.* (*subjective/nominative, objective, possessive*). Some have different forms for each case.

3. Be *personal* and refer to people or things. (*I, you, they, him her it...*)

4. Be *relative* and introduce certain *noun* and *adjective clauses.* (*who/whose/whom, which, what, that*)

5. Be *interrogative* and introduce a question. (*who/whose/whom, which, what?*)

6. Be *demonstrative* and point out the antecedent. (*this, these*; *that, those*)

7. Be *reflexive* or *intensive* and reflect back to or intensify the antecedent. (*myself, yourself, himself, herself, itself, ourselves, yourselves, themselves*)

8. Be *reciprocal* and refer to individual parts of a plural antecedent. (*each other*)

9. Be *indefinite* and refer to non-specific things or people. (*any, each, some, anyone/body/thing, everyone/body/thing, someone/body/thing...*)

Decision tree for analyzing the ten English noun roles

Figure III: Noun Roles
!
! (Modifier)->
!
————————!->(Always Pre-modifier, Same or Different Referent,
! (Head   !   Never Separated from HW by Mandatory
V word)   !   Pause)NOUN ADJUNCT-Noun Used as Adjective.
!   V
! (Pre- or Post-modifier; same Referent Always; Separated from HW by
   mandatory pause. Always in the pre-position
! Post-Position Usually NOUN IN APPOSITION
!
! (Non-Pronoun Function)—>
!
————————————————!——>(Name, Pronoun or Title,
! (Pronoun Referent)   !   Used to Draw Attention)
V   V   VOCATIVE—Noun Used in
! (Adverbial Referent) ADVERBIAL   Direct Address.
! OBJECT—Noun Used as an Adverb
!
! (Non-Complement)————>
!
————————————————!->   (After and Governed by Preposition)
! (Complement)   !   OBJECT OF PREPOSITION
V   V
!   (Otherwise) SUBJECT
!
! (Single Complement)————->
!

```
————————————————--!->(Complement of Linking Verb)
! (Double Complement)      !    PREDICATE NOMINATIVE
V                          V
!  Complement of Transitive
!  Verb) DIRECT OBJECT
!
! (Same Referent Complements)—————>
!
——————————————

! (Different Referent Complements)        !
V                                         !
!————!                                    !
        V                                 V
   ———————-                          ———————-
   !         !                       !          !
INDIRECT  DIRECT                  DIRECT      OBJECT
OBJECT    OBJECT                  OBJECT      COMPLEMENT
```

WHAT CONJUNCTIONS CAN DO:

1. Connect words, phrases, and clauses.

Our petitions^{Sb} have been slighted; our remonstrances^{Sb} have produced additional violence^{DO} and insult;^{DO} our supplications^{Sb} have been disregarded; and we^{Sb} have been spurned, with contempt,^{OP} from the foot^{OP} of the throne!^{OP} In vain,^{OP} after these things,^{OP} may we^{Sb} indulge the fond hope^{DO} of peace^{OP} and reconciliation.^{OP}

—P. Henry

2. Coordinating conjunctions connect two grammatically equivalent structures:

      A. addition—*and*
      B. contrast—*but, yet*
      C. result or effect—*so*
      D. reason or cause—*for*
      E. choice—*or*
      F. negative choice—*nor*

3. Correlative conjunctions function in pairs to join equivalent grammatical structures.

      A. *both...and*
      B. *either...or*
      C. *neither...nor*
      D. *not only...but (also)*
      E. *whether...or*
      F. *not...so much as*

4. Subordinating conjunctions introduce DEPENDENT CLAUSES, structures that are grammatically less important than those in an INDEPENDENT CLAUSE in the same sentence.

    A. time—*after, before, once, since, until, while*
    B. reason or cause—*as, because, since*
    C. result or effect—*in order that, so, so that, that*
    D. condition—*if, even if, provided that, unless*
    E. contrast—*although, even though, though, whereas*
    F. choice -*rather than, than, whether*

Clauses that start with subordinating conjunctions are adverb clauses, functioning as adverbs and usually answering some question about the independent clause such as *how? why? when? under what circumstances?* BUT adverb clauses can modify verbs, adjectives, and other adverbs, as well as entire independent clauses. (Less frequently, they may function as nouns also: "<u>Whether he will agree</u> is uncertain.")

Shall we acquire the means of <u>effectual</u> resistance by lying *supinely* on <u>our</u> backs and hugging the <u>delusive</u> phantom of hope, *until <u>our</u> enemies shall have bound us hand and foot?*

                                        -P. Henry

WHAT VERBS CAN DO

1. Convey information about what is happening, what will happen, what has happened.

No man thinks more highly than I do of the patriotism, as well as abilities, of the very worthy gentlemen who have just addressed the house.

—P. Henry

I <u>teach </u>the class every evening.
I <u>taught</u> my class last night.
I <u>will teach</u> it again tomorrow night.

2. Convey person speaking or experiencing action—1st, 2nd, 3rd.

And judging by the past, I <u>wish</u> to know what there <u>has</u> *been* in the conduct of the British ministry for the last ten years to justify those hopes with which gentlemen <u>have</u> been *pleased* to solace themselves and the House.

—P. Henry

<u>I like</u> the class.
<u>You would like</u> the class.
<u>She likes</u> the class
<u>The students like</u> the class.

3. Convey number of people acting or experiencing—singular, plural. (Have different form or ending for plural.)

But different men often see the same subject in different lights;

—P. Henry

> *I laugh often in class.*
> *John laughs often.*
> *We laugh a lot.*

4. Convey tense when an action occurs -past, present, future. (Have different form or ending, and/or employ auxiliary verb to indicate difference.)

And, therefore, I hope it will not be thought disrespectful to those gentlemen if, entertaining as I do, opinions of a character very opposite to theirs, I shall speak forth my sentiments freely and without reserve.

—P. Henry

> *We tried to keep things light in the beginning.*
> *We try to do that now.*
> *We will be able to try until the end.*

5. Convey mood-information about what attitude is expressed toward the action-indicative, imperative, subjunctive.

Forbid it, Almighty God! I know not what course others may take; but as for me, give me liberty or give me death!

—P. Henry

> *Sometimes it is hard to stay attentive.*
> *You have to stay attentive!*
> *If the class were shorter, attention would be easier.*

6. Convey voice—whether the subject acts or is acted on—active voice or passive voice. (Employ auxiliary verbs to convey passive voice.)

<u>Our</u> chains are forged!

—P. Henry

At least the class <u>is</u> interactive.
Students <u>are</u> not just <u>lectured</u> by the teacher.

7. Pretend to be nouns by dressing as gerunds using the "-ing" form. (Called a verbal in this form. Can have objects. Can only be a noun.)

<u>Learning</u> is sometimes painful.
<u>Teaching</u> is tiresome as well.
<u>Learning grammar</u> is especially hard.
<u>Teaching grammar</u> to tired students is hard also.

8. Pretend to be nouns by teaming up with to and dressing as an infinitive. (Also called a verbal. Can have an object. Can be an adjective or adverb as well as a noun.)

It is in vain, sir, <u>to extenuate the matter</u>.

—P. Henry

<u>To learn grammar</u> is an accomplishment.
The trick is <u>to learn</u> well.

9. Pretend to be adjectives by dressing as present participles. (Also called a verbal. Also use the "-ing" form. Have to modify a nearby noun.)

But different men often see the same subject in different lights; and, therefore, I hope it will not be thought disrespectful to those gentlemen if, *entertaining as I do*, opinions of a character very opposite to theirs, I shall speak forth my sentiments freely and without reserve.

—P. Henry

<u>Learning too late</u>, he failed the course.
The students, <u>learning through practice</u>, soon mastered grammar.

10. Pretend to be adjectives by dressing as past participles. (Also called a verbal. Use the "-ed" or the irregular form. Have to modify a nearby noun.)

<u>Learned societies</u> are very exclusive.
"<u>Learned helplessness</u>" is a psychological term

WHAT TYPES VERBS CAN BE:

1. Main verb—conveys main action, occurrence, or state of being.

2. Linking verb—conveys a state of being (is), relates to the senses (tastes), or indicates a condition (grows). Also joins a subject to the word/words that rename/describe it. (<u>Caution: sense and condition verbs may or may not be linking. If you can substitute was/were for them and have the sentence make sense, they ARE linking.</u>)

3. Auxiliary verb—a verb employed by the main verb to convey information about tense, mood, voice. Modal auxiliary verbs include can/could, may/might, shall/should, will/would, must as well as others that add possibility or ability to verbs. Other auxiliary verbs include do/does/did/done, be/am/is/are/was/were/been, have/has/had when combined with other verbs.

   He did see them.
   They are working.
   She has seen the light.

4. Transitive verb—must be followed by a direct object.

5. Intransitive verb—does not have a direct object.

WHAT ADVERBS CAN DO!

1. Adverbs modify other words—<u>*verbs, adverbs, adjectives, independent clauses, (nouns in special cases).*</u>

If we were <u>base</u> *enough* to desire it, it is now *too late* to retire from <u>the</u> contest.

—P. Henry

2. Sometimes they end in "ly", but not always. (Sometimes adjectives end in "ly"—lovely)

Besides, sir, we shall *not* fight <u>our </u>battles *alone*.

—P. Henry

3. Many have positive, comparative, and superlative forms just like adjectives. Same rules apply…

far, farther, farthest.

4. *Descriptive* adverbs show level of intensity for actions.

happy, happier, happiest.

5. *Conjunctive* adverbs modify by creating logical connections in meaning.

> A. addition—*also, furthermore, moreover, besides.*
> B. contrast—*however, still, nevertheless, conversely, nonetheless, instead, otherwise.*
> C. comparison—*similarly, likewise.*
> D. result or summary—*therefore, thus, consequently, accordingly, hence, then.*
> E. time—*next, then, meanwhile, finally, subsequently.*
> F. emphasis—*indeed, certainly.*

6. *Relative* adverbs are words like *where, when, how, why* used to introduce <u>adjective clauses</u>.

7. <u>Whole phrases and clauses can act like adverbs!</u>

More about Adverbs:

In traditional grammar (Hartwell's grammar 4), adverbs, not modifying adjectives, adverbs, (and less often nouns) are considered verb modifiers, not complements. In most modern scientific grammars (Hartwell's grammar 2), adverbs may be complements.

Rather than some abstract explanation as to why this is, some examples of adverb parallels with adjective complements are shown below.

It is <u>slow</u>. (adjective)   *How <u>slow</u> is it?*
It moved <u>slowly</u>. (adverb)   *How <u>slowly</u> did it move?*

They looked <u>good</u>. (adjective)   *How <u>good</u> did they look?*
They worked <u>well</u>. (adverb)   *How well did they work?*

I found her <u>abrupt</u>. (adj.)   *How <u>abrupt</u> did I find her?*
I found her <u>abruptly</u>. (adv.)   *How <u>abruptly</u> did I find her?*

The lock worked <u>loose</u>. (adj.)   *How <u>loose</u> did the lock work?*

The lock worked <u>loosely</u>. (adv.)   *How <u>loosely</u> did the lock work?*

The shift workers will make the day <u>short</u>. (adjective)   *How <u>short</u> will the shift workers make the day?*

The shift workers will end the day <u>shortly</u>. (adverb)   *How <u>shortly</u> will the shift workers end the day?*

ANY GROUP OF WORDS—WHICH CAN ANSWER THE QUESTIONS: HOW,
WHEN, WHERE, AND WHY [UNLESS IT MODIFIES A NOUN]—IS USED AS
AN ADVERB: (ADVERBIAL)

Figure IV.

We need the money <u>to buy presents</u>.   Form: Infinitive
Why [do we need the money?]   Function: Adverb

He'll end it <u>whatever day it is.</u>   Form: Relative
                                                      Pronoun
                                                      Clause
When [will he end it?]   Function: Adverb

She won the contest, <u>doing her best.</u>   Form: Present
                                                      Participle
                                                      Phrase
How [did she win the contest?]   Function: Adverb

They walked <u>home.</u>   Form
Where [did they walk?]   Function: Adverb

I did it <u>my way.</u>   Form: Noun Phrase
How [did I do it?]   Function: Adverb

She discarded it <u>because it was torn.</u> Form: Subordinate

                                                      Clause

Why [did she discard it?]   Function: Adverb

You will know it <u>when it happens.</u>   Form: Relative
                                                      Adverb
                                                      Clause
When [will you know it?]   Function: Adverb

WHAT ADJECTIVES CAN DO

1. **Adjectives** are words or groups of words that describe other words—nouns and pronouns.

If we wish to be <u>free</u>—if we mean to preserve *inviolate* <u>those</u> <u>inestimable</u> privileges for which we have been *so long* contending—if we mean *not basely* to abandon <u>the</u> <u>noble</u> struggle in which we have been *so long* engaged, and which we have pledged ourselves *never* to abandon until <u>the</u> <u>glorious</u> object of <u>our</u> contest shall be obtained—we must fight! I repeat it, sir, we must fight!

—P. Henry

2. They can be complements after linking verbs. (Only "bad" is correct after a linking verb—not "badly".)

Justice is blind.
The detective looked cautious.

3. They can have "positive", "comparative", and "superlative" forms:
        A. 1-syllable == *er, est.*
        B. 3-syllables == *more, most, less, least.*
        C. 2-syllables == can be either…

4. Sometimes nouns modify other nouns—"truck driver"—but generally only in familiar terms.

5. Descriptive adjectives show levels of intensity by using the different forms.

Worse, worse, worst.
Good, better, best.

6. Proper adjectives are formed from proper noun by adding inflected endings- ful, an, ish, less, like.

A Patrick Henry-like patriot.

7. Limiting adjectives or determiners convey whether nouns are general or specific, how many there are, which one it is.
   A. articles—a, an, the.
   B. demonstrative—this, these, that, those.
   C. indefinite—any, each, few, other, some.
   D. interrogative—what, which, whose.
   E. numerical—one, first, two, second.
   F. possessive—my, your, their, and others.
   G. relative—what, which, whose, whatever, and others.

8. <u>Whole phrases and clauses can act like adjectives and modify nouns.</u>

ANY GROUP OF WORDS—WHICH MODIFIES A NOUN OR PRONOUN [EXCEPT A FOLLOWING NOUN OR NOUN PHRASE THAT RENAMES THE NOUN]—IS USED AS AN ADJECTIVE: (ADJECTIVAL)

Figure V.

It is time <u>to leave.</u>	Form:	Infinitive
	Function:	Adjective
The car <u>that he drove</u> is expensive.	Form:	Relative Pronoun Clause
	Function:	Adjective
The men <u>working at the plant</u> were mad.	Form:	Present Participle Phrase
	Function:	Adjective
The <u>truck</u> driver saw him.	Form:	Noun
	Function:	Adjective
The <u>dog and pony</u> show was over.	Form:	Noun Phrase
	Function:	Adjective
The day <u>after the storm</u> was messy	Form:	Subordinate Clause
	Function:	Adjective
The cabin <u>where we stayed</u> was quaint.	Form:	Relative Adverb Clause
	Function:	Adjective

WHAT PREPOSITIONS DO:

Prepositions begin prepositional phrases that function as adjectives or adverbs.

They must be memorized.

Some words which begin prepositional phrases may occur before a subject-predicate set; in which case they are functioning as subordinate conjunctions, not prepositions.

about the book

above my head

across the street

after the rain

against the odds

along the sidewalk

amid the crowd

among our group

around the bend

at her dentist

before then

behind it

below ground

beneath contempt

beside himself

between jobs

beyond its bounds

but him (but = except)

by now

down those stairs

during the war

except her son

for certain

from the mall

in action

into the breach

like new

of mice and men

off duty

on time

over the top

past the White House

through the woods

throughout her term

to arms

toward the left

under siege

underneath the roof

until tomorrow

unto others

up above

upon reflection

within the circle

with malice

without a doubt

WHAT INTERJECTIONS DO:

Interjections are words or expressions that convey surprise or another strong emotion. Alone, an interjection is usually punctuated with an exclamation point. As part of a sentence, an interjection is set off by a comma.

English Sentence Constituents and Modifiers:

the Sentence itself   S

the Non-Modifying	Subject	Sb.
(Headword)	Object of Preposition	OP
Noun Roles:	Predicate Nominative	PN
	Direct Object	DO
	Indirect Object	IO
	Object Complement Noun	OCN

(The other four roles would fall under the modifiers)

(Headword)	Predicate Adjective	PA
Adjective Roles:	Object Complement Adjective	OCA

Sentence	(words like interjections & conjunctive	
Modifier	adverbs, ANY word group that modifies	
	the whole sentence rather than any part,	
	e.g. absolute constructions, direct address)	SM

Noun Modifiers—Items usually Adjectival in function

Verb Modifiers—Items usually Adverbial in function

Adjective Modifiers— limit or enhance nouns and pronouns

Adverb Modifiers— limit or enhance verbs, other adverbs or adjectives

<u>English Constructions/Forms/Clusters/Phrases/Word Groups:</u>

sentence	= subject	+ predicate	S
subordinate clause	= subordinate conjunction	+ sentence	SC
relative (pronoun) clause	= relative pronoun	+ sentence (sometimes predicate)	RP
relative (adverb) clause	= relative adverb	+ sentence	RA
infinitive	= preposition "to"	+ verb phrase with leftmost verbal element in base form	I
prepositional phrase	= preposition	+ pronoun/noun/noun phrase usually, occasionally adverb/adverb phrase, rarely—mostly with prepositions "for" and "like."—adjective/	PP

adjective phrase

verb phrase	= construction with verb as		VP

	ultimate headword	
noun phrase	= construction with noun/pronoun as ultimate headword	NP
adjective phrase	= construction with adjective as ultimate headword	AjP
adverb phrase	= construction with adverb as ultimate headword	AvP

Functions:

Verbal	= A verb or verb phrase which EITHER is a predicate OR is the second part of an infinitive.	V
Nominal	= ANY word or construction which can take a personal or demonstrative pronoun as a substitute.	N
Adverbial	= ANY word or construction which answers the questions "how, when, where" or "why" UNLESS the word or construction is modifying a noun.	Av
Adjectival	= ANY word or construction which modifies a noun.	Aj
Sentence	= A sentence itself is a form, function, and constituent.	S

Chapter III

DIAGRAMING SAMPLES

Sentence Clause Types:

A simple sentence has only one subject and predicate set. (one clause)

The tall old aging aged gray stone houses listed in the directory have fallen

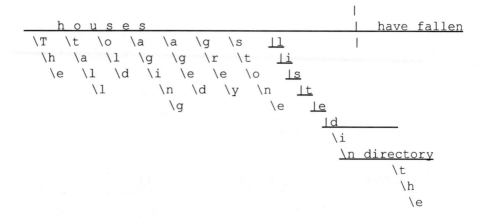

```
                                                    |
         h  o  u  s  e  s                           |   have fallen
  \T   \t   \o   \a   \a   \g   \s    |l             |
  \h   \a   \l   \g   \g   \r   \t    |i
  \e   \l   \d   \i   \e   \e   \o    |s
        \l           \n   \d   \y   \n   |t
             \g                \e    |e
                                        |d
                                     \i
                                     \n directory
                                        \t
                                        \h
                                        \e
```

He could not have been more helpful in this case

```
       |                    \
He  |  could have been  \  helpful.
    |  \n       \i           \m
       \o       \n   case.    \o
         \t          \t        \r
                     \h         \e
                     \i
                     \s
```

Doing all this work will increase our productivity.

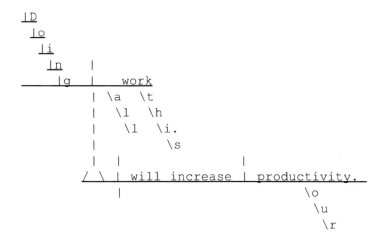

A compound sentence has at least two subject and predicate sets, (two clauses or more) and both, or all, sets must be independent/main clauses

It is important to finish the project; therefore, we should have more staff for the duration of the work.

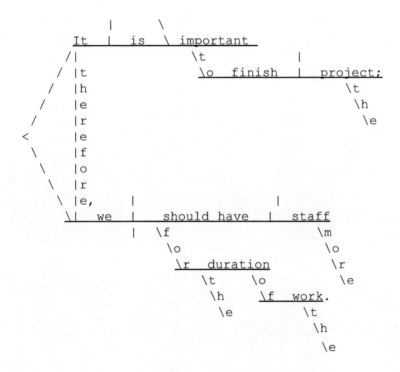

Making that choice was right; everyone agreed with his decision, and
we agree as well.

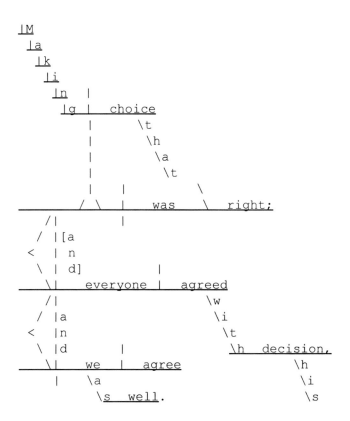

To help him was our goal, but winning is really another matter.

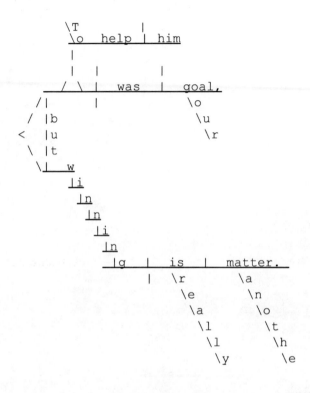

A complex sentence has at least two subject and predicate sets, (two clauses or more) but only one of the sets can be an independent/main clause.

Whatever is necessary will be accomplished.

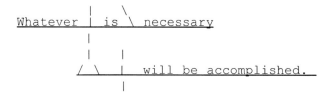

They attempted to do the best that they could because they wanted to get a good grade

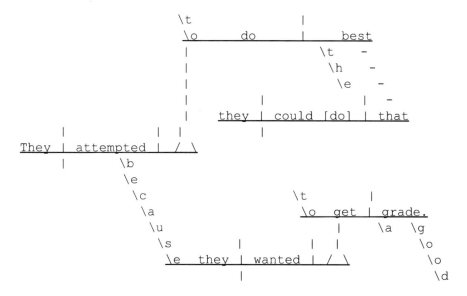

The people whom we met were very interesting and very lively.

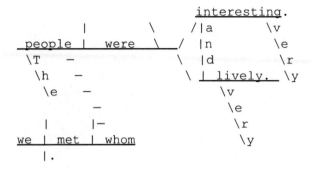

A compound-complex sentence has at least 3 subject and predicate sets.(3 clauses.) At least 2 must be independent/main clauses, and at least one (or more) must be a dependent clause.

Working with these excellent authors was exciting, and I hope that I will get the opportunity to do it again

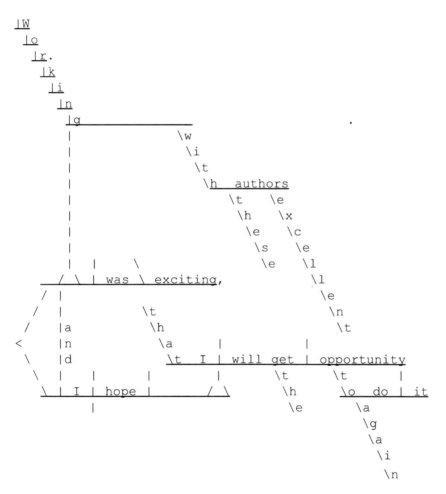

He knew what he had to do, he did what was necessary, and he finished what he had started.

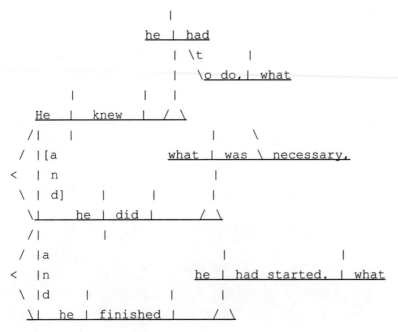

Because I preferred the former and did not hesitate
to express this fact, an argument ensued, and I left.

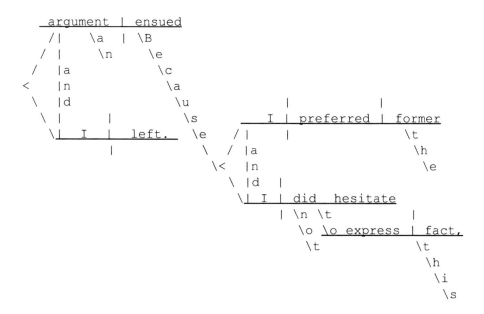

Sentence Complement Types:

Intransitive (No Noun, Pronoun or Adjective Complement, An
Adverbial Modifier possible. Either a linking or a Non-linking Verb
Predicate.)

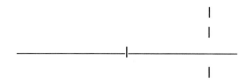

Joe agrees.

```
       |
Joe  |  agrees.
       |
```

That all the volunteers arrived early helped greatly.

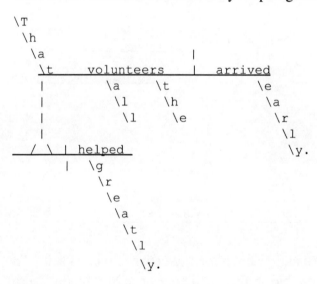

He stopped when it was over.

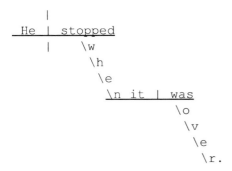

```
        |
  He  |  stopped
        |      \w
              \h
               \e
                 \n  it  |  was
                             \o
                              \v
                               \e
                                \r.
```

I left after dinner.

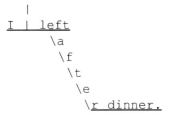

```
        |
 I  |  left
        \a
         \f
          \t
           \e
             \r  dinner.
```

Whatever he did worked.

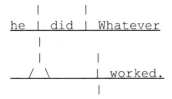

```
       |          |
 he  |  did  |  Whatever
       |
       |          |
    /  \          |  worked.
       |
```

Mary is here.

```
Mary | is
      | \   here.
```

To do it well is recommended.

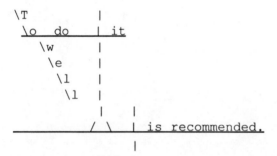

```
\T            |
 \o   do  | it
   \w         |
    \e        |
     \l       |
      \l      |
           |   |
_____/ \ | is recommended.
           |
```

Subject Complement: Two Subtypes—
Predicate Adjective, Predicate Nominative.

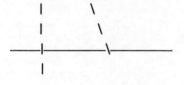

Predicate Adjective (An Adjective Complement alone or in a phrase, referring back to the Subject after a linking Verb or a Non-Linking Verb with the sense of a Linking Verb.)

Joe is tall.

```
       |      \
Joe |  is  \  tall.  
       |
```

The weather turned cold.

```
          |            \
weather |  turned  \  cold.  
     \T         |
       \h
         \e
```

Mary became wealthier than Sam.

```
        |            \
Mary |  became  \  wealthier
        |                        \t
                                   \h
                                     \a
                                       \n    Sam.
```

What they did was excellent.

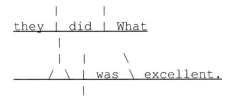

```
        |        |
they |  did  |  What
         |
         |    |       \
    ____/ \ |  was  \  excellent.  
              |
```

The promise rang true.

```
        |         \
promise | rang  \ true.
      \T |
        \h
          \e
```

He sounded good.

```
    |           \
He  | sounded \ good.
    |
```

Predicate Nominative: (A Pronoun or Noun Complement alone or in a phrase, referring back to the Subject after a Linking Verb.)

It was just what I said.

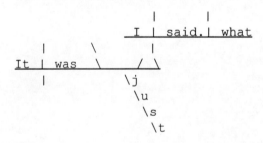

John became a leader.

```
      |          \
John | became  \ leader.
      |                \a
```

Ending it seemed the solution.

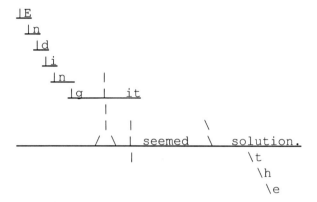

How it happened today appears the norm for the situation.

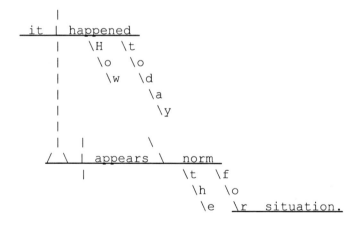

Direct Object: (A Pronoun or Noun Complement alone or in a phrase, not referring back to the Subject, and after a non-Linking Verb)

Ending it effected the solution.

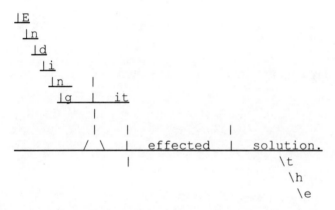

John saw the leader.

```
         |       |
John  |  saw  |  leader.
         |         \t
                   \h
                   \e
```

How it happened today established the norm for the situation.

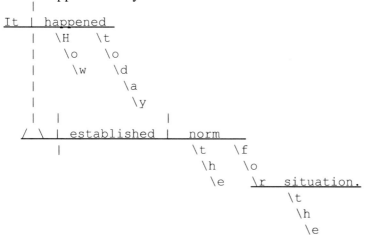

```
                   |
     It  |  happened
          |    \H     \t
          |     \o     \o
          |      \w     \d
          |            \a
          |             \y
       |   |                |
      / \  | established |   norm
          |              \t     \f
                         \h     \o
                          \e    \r   situation.
                                     \t
                                     \h
                                      \e
```

He did just what I said.

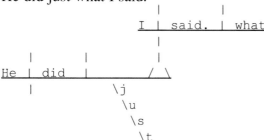

```
                     |              |
                 I  |  said.  |  what
                     |
       |     |        |
     He  |  did  |          / \
       |          \j
                 \u
                 \s
                 \t
```

Indirect Object: (Two separate Noun Complements or groups of words which function as such—not referring to the subject or to each other—following a non-linking Verb.)

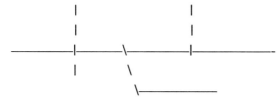

She asked us a question.

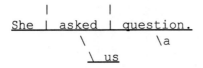

```
        |           |
She | asked | question.
         \           \a
          \ us
```

We told them what we knew.

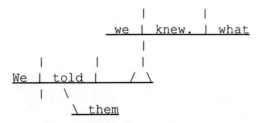

```
                   |          |
               we | knew. | what
                            |
     |        |        |
We | told |      / \
     |   \
          \ them
```

I brought him the book.

```
     |               |
I | brought | book.
     |    \            \t
          \ him       \h
                       \e
```

What happened gave people a new perspective.

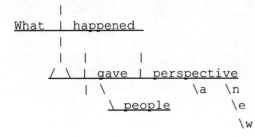

```
        |
What   | happened
        |
        |   |        |
      / \ | gave | perspective
        | \             \a    \n
          \ people        \e
                           \w
```

Playing well assured her a victory.

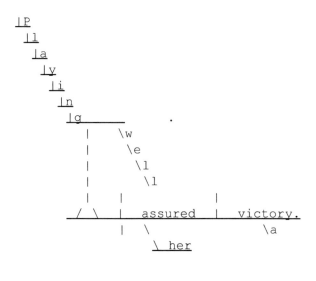

Object Complement: Two Subtypes—Object Complement Noun &
Object Complement Adjective.

Object Complement Noun: (Two separate Noun Complements or
groups of words which function as such—not referring to the Subject,
but sharing the same referent—following
a non-Linking Verb.)

She named the baby Ruth.

```
        |          |       \
She  |  named  |  baby  \  Ruth
        |                \t
                         \h
                          \e
```

The people elected John the mayor of the city.

```
           |          |        \
people  |  elected  |  John  \  mayor
   \T      |                   \t   \o
    \h                          \h   \f   city.
     \e.                         \e       \t
                                           \h
                                            \e
```

The clothes store called the final dress sale a success.

```
            |          |            \
  store  |  called  |     sale     \  success.
  \T     \c   |              \t   \f   \d        \a
   \h     \l                  \h   \i   \r
    \e     \o                  \e   \n   \e
            \t                      \a   \s
             \h                      \l   \s
              \e
               \s
```

Object Complement Adjective: (A Noun Complement and an Adjective Complement or groups of words which function as such—not referring to the Subject, but sharing the same referent as the Direct Object—-following a non-Linking Verb.)

The arctic air fronts turned the local weather cold.

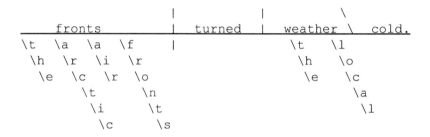

```
                          |            |         \
____fronts_____|__turned____|__weather_\__cold.
\t   \a   \a   \f         |             \t    \l
  \h   \r   \i   \r                       \h    \o
    \e   \c   \r   \o                       \e    \c
           \t         \n                           \a
           \i         \t                           \l
             \c         \s
```

The spicy food made him ill.

```
             |          |        \
____food_____|__made____|__him___\__ill.
  \T   \s   |
    \h   \p
      \e   \i
             \c
             \y
```

The homeowners kept their neighborhood clean.

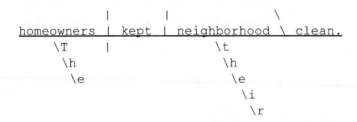

```
                |          |              \
homeowners  |  kept  |  neighborhood  \  clean.
     \T         |                   \t
      \h                             \h
       \e                             \e
                                       \i
                                        \r
```

Expletive Sentence: {Some think that this is an inverted form of a specialized Intransitive Sentence. "There" is followed by a Linking Verb Predicate—no complement—followed by a SUBJECT, NOT a PREDICATE NOMINATIVE.)

```
              (There)
                 |
                 |
    ─────────────|─────────
                 |
```

There are no exceptions in this matter.

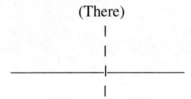

```
          (There)
             |
exceptions   |    are
    \n       |    \i
     \o           \n   matter.
                   \t
                    \h
                     \i
                      \s
```

There appears to be some solution.

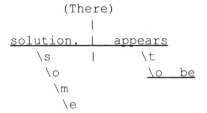

```
          (There)
             |
solution. |   appears
    \s      |     \t
     \o           \o   be
      \m
       \e
```

There has arisen a necessity to continue.

```
          (There)
             |
necessity  |   has arisen
   \a    \t |
           \o   continue.
```

Chapter IV

LESSON PLAN FORMAT

We advise the assignment of several lesson plans for grammar during the course of any methods course. Here is a lesson plan format that has all the standard components.

LESSON PLAN #

TITLE:_____

AUTHOR:_____

GRADE LEVEL/SUBJECT:_____

OBJECTIVE(s): "Students/pupils will learn/demonstrate…"

_____

_____

_____

_____

_____

_____

_____

ACTIVITIES AND PROCEDURES:

_____
_____
_____
_____
_____
_____
_____
_____
_____

EVALUATION:

_____
_____
_____
_____
_____
_____
_____
_____
_____

Chapter V

MATERIALS FOR
GRAMMATICAL ANALYSIS

We have selected some famous speeches for your use to label for grammatical function, for sentence type, or for any other grammatical purpose. The texts of these speeches were pulled from the Internet. Websites are credited.

It is our recommendation that students hand copy short pieces of text from those speeches to use for various sorts of labeling. This seems to reinforce needed skills.

The text of the speech by Patrick Henry to follow will be the basis for various analyses. These mix familiar and traditional presentation and nomenclature with insights from structural and generative grammar. They reflect what worked rather than what is current, fashionable or revered past practice.

The first two sentences, analyzed as thoroughly as this treatment's scope permits, will be copied and dissected after the speech. The text portion of the speech will be unmarked.

The remaining first and next two paragraphs have the predicate's marker and main verb respectively underlined and italicized in the text itself.

The fourth paragraph marks noun roles in superscripts. Only individual nouns and pronouns are marked. Word groups and other parts of speech functioning as nouns are unmarked. Noun role abbreviations are found in the examples for noun roles' section, earlier in the text. Asterisks mark Direct Objects that are semantic subjects of infinitive, non-finite, verbal forms.

The fifth paragraph underlines individual adjectives and italicizes individual adverbs. Other words or word groups functioning as adjectives or adverbs are unmarked.

The final paragraph is diagrammed following the analysis of the first two sentences of the first paragraph.

March 23, 1775, Give Me Liberty or Give Me Death, By Patrick Henry

No man thinks more highly than I do of the patriotism, as well as abilities, of the very worthy gentlemen who have just addressed the house. But different men often see the same subject in different lights; and, therefore, I hope it will not be thought disrespectful to those gentlemen if, entertaining as I do opinions of a character very opposite to theirs, I shall speak forth my sentiments freely and without reserve. This *is* no time for ceremony. The question before the house *is* one of awful moment to this country. For my own part, I *consider* it as nothing less than a question of freedom or slavery; and in proportion to the magnitude of the subject <u>ought to</u> *be* the freedom of the debate. It is only in this way that we <u>can</u> *hope* to arrive at the truth, and fulfill the great responsibility which we *hold* to God and our country. <u>Should</u> I *keep* back my opinions at such a time, through fear of giving offense, I <u>should</u> *consider* myself as guilty of treason towards my country, and of an act of disloyalty toward the Majesty of Heaven, which I <u>*revere*</u> above all earthly kings.

Mr. President, it <u>*is*</u> natural to man to indulge in the illusions of hope. We <u>*are*</u> apt to shut our eyes against a painful truth, and listen to the song of that siren till she <u>*transforms*</u> us into beasts. Is this the part of wise men, engaged in a great and arduous struggle for liberty? <u>Are</u> we *disposed* to be of the numbers of those who, having eyes, see not, and, having ears, hear not, the things which so nearly <u>*concern*</u> their temporal salvation? For my part, whatever anguish of spirit it <u>may</u> *cost*, I <u>am</u> *willing* to know the whole truth, to know the worst, and to provide for it.

I <u>*have*</u> but one lamp by which my feet <u>are</u> *guided*, and that <u>*is*</u> the lamp of experience. I <u>*know*</u> of no way of judging of the future but by the past. And judging by the past, I <u>*wish*</u> to know what there <u>has</u> *been* in the conduct of the British ministry for the last ten years to justify those hopes with which gentlemen <u>have</u> been *pleased* to solace themselves and the House. <u>*Is*</u> it that insidious smile with which our petition <u>has</u> been lately *received*?

Trust <u>it</u>[DO] not, sir;[DA] it[Sb] will prove a snare to your feet.[OP] Suffer not yourselves[DO] to be betrayed with a kiss.[OP] Ask yourselves[DO] how this gracious reception[Sb] of our petition[OP] comports with those warlike preparations[OP] which cover our waters[DO] and darken our land.[DO] Are fleets[Sb] and armies[Sb] necessary to a work[OP] of love[OP] and reconciliation?[OP]

Have we[Sb] shown ourselves* so unwilling to be reconciled that force[Sb] must be called in to win back our love?[DO] Let us* not deceive ourselves,[DO] sir.[DA] These[Sb] are the implements[PN] of war[OP] and subjuga-tion;[OP] the last argu-ments[PN] to which kings[Sb] resort. I[Sb] ask gentlemen,[DO] sir,[DA] what means this martial array,[Sb] if its purpose be not to force us[DO] to submission?[OP] Can gentlemen[Sb] assign any other possible motive[DO] for it?[OP] Has Great Britain[Sb] any enemy,[DO] in this quarter[OP] of the world,[OP] to call for all this accumulation[OP] of navies[OP] and armies?[OP] No, sir,[DA] she has none.[DO] They[Sb] are meant for us:OP theySb can be meant for no other.OP TheySb are sent over to bind and rivet upon us[OP] those chains[DO] which the British ministry[Sb] have been so long forging. And what have we[Sb] to oppose to them?[OP] Shall we[Sb] try argument?[DO] Sir,[DA] we[Sb] have been trying that[DO] for the last ten years.[OP] Have we[Sb] anything new[DO] to offer upon the subject?[OP] Nothing.[DO] We[Sb] have held the subject[DO] up in every light[OP] of which it[Sb] is capable; but it[Sb] has been all in vain.[OP] Shall we[Sb] resort to entreaty[OP] and humble supplication?[OB] What terms[DO] shall weSb find which have not been already exhausted? Let us* not, I beseech you,[DO] sir,[DA] deceive ourselves.[DO] Sir,[DA] we[Sb] have done everything[DO] that could be done to avert the storm[DO] which is now coming on. We[Sb] have petitioned; we[Sb] have remonstrated; we[Sb] have supplicated; we[Sb] have prostrated ourselves[DO] before the throne,[OP] and have implored its interposition* to arrest the tyrannical hands[DO] of the ministry[OP] and Parliament.[OP] Our petitions[Sb] have been slighted; our remonstrances[Sb] have produced additional violence[DO] and insult;[DO] our supplications[Sb] have been disregarded; and we[Sb] have been spurned, with contempt,[OP] from the foot[OP] of the throne![OP] In vain,[OP] after these things,[OP] may we[Sb] indulge the fond hope[DO] of peace[OP] and reconciliation.[OP]

There is *no longer* <u>any</u> room for hope. If we wish to be <u>free</u>—if we mean to preserve *inviolate* <u>those</u> <u>inestimable</u> privileges for which we have been *so long* contending—if we mean *not basely* to abandon <u>the</u> <u>noble</u> struggle in which we have been *so long* engaged, and which we have pledged ourselves *never* to abandon until the glorious object of our contest shall be obtained—we must fight! I repeat it, sir, we must fight! An appeal to arms and to the God of hosts is all that is left us! They tell us, sir, that we are weak; unable to cope with *so* formidable an adversary. But when shall we be stronger? Will it be the next week, or the next year? Will it be when we are *totally* disarmed, and when a British guard shall be stationed in every house? Shall we gather strength but irresolution and inaction? Shall we acquire the means of ef-fectual resistance by lying *supinely* on our backs and hugging the delusive phantom of hope, until our enemies shall have bound us hand and foot? Sir, we are *not* weak if we make a proper use of those means which the God of nature hath placed in our power. The millions of people, armed in the holy cause of liberty, and in such a country as that which we possess, are invincible by any force which our enemy can send against us. *Besides*, sir, we shall *not* fight our battles *alone*. There is a just God who presides over the destinies of nations, and who will raise up friends to fight our battles for us. The battle, sir, is *not* to the strong *alone*; it is to the vigilant, the active, the brave. *Besides*, sir, we have no election. If we were base *enough* to desire it, it is now *too late* to retire from the contest. There is no retreat but in submission and slavery! Our chains are forged! Their clanking may be heard on the plains of Boston! The war is inevitable—and let it come! I repeat it, sir, let it come.

Sir,[DA] we[Sb] have done everything[DO] that could be done to avert the storm[DO] which is now coming on. Trust it[DO] not, sir;[DA] it[Sb] will prove a snare to your feet.[OP] Gentlemen may cry, Peace, Peace—but there is no peace. The war is actually begun! The next gale that sweeps from the north will bring to our ears the clash of resounding arms! Our brethren are already in the field! Why stand we here idle? What is it that gentlemen wish? What would they have? Is life so dear, or peace so sweet, as to be purchased at the price of chains and slavery? Forbid it,

Almighty God! I know not what course others may take; but as for me, give me liberty or give me death!

http://www.law.ou.edu/ushist.html

March 23,1775, Give Me Liberty or Give Me Death,
By
Patrick (First two Sentences Analyzed Fully) [Reader Advisory:
Henry   not for the grammatically faint-hearted.)

First Line: Sentence Constitutent: A Sentence itself, one of
                       6 Noun or 2 Adjective Roles; A Predicate; or
                       Modifier of a Sentence or a Nominal, Verbal,
                       Adjectival or Adverbial: 14 Choices.

Second Line: Word Group, Form: Sentence; Subordinate or
                       Relative Pronoun/Adverb Clause; Infinitive;
                       Prepositional, Noun, Verb, Adjective or Adverb
                       Phrase: 10 Choices.

Third Line: Word Group, Function: Sentence, Nominal,
                       Verbal, Adjectival and Adverbial: 5 Choices.

Fourth Line: Division into two parts; either a function, repeat-
                       ing the possibilities of the above line or one of
                       the eight parts of speech: 13 Choices [Actually
                       more than that occur, as many sub-classes of
                       parts of speech have their own designation.]
(Note: Sentence can occupy any of the four lines)

No man thinks more highly than I do of the patriotism, as well as abilities, of the very worthy gentlemen who have just addressed the house. But different men often see the same subject in different lights; and, therefore, I hope it will not be thought disrespectful to those gentlemen if, entertaining as I do opinions of a character very opposite to theirs, I shall speak forth my sentiments freely and without reserve.

(Compound) Sentence

Sentence
Sentence
Sentence
(Sentence and Sentence)

———

No man thinks more highly than I do of the patriotism, as well as abilities, of the very worthy gentlemen who have just addressed the house.

Sentence
Sentence
Sentence
([Subject:]Nominal and [Predicate] Verbal)

———

"No man"

Subject
Noun Phrase
Nominal

([Limiting] <u>Adjective</u> and <u>Noun</u>)

"<u>thinks</u> <u>more highly than I do of the patriotism,
as well as abilities of the very worthy gentlemen
who have just addressed the house.</u>"

Predicate
Verb Phrase
Verbal
(<u>Verb</u> and <u>Adverbial</u>)

_____

"<u>more highly than I do</u> of the patriotism, as well as
abilities of the very worthy gentlemen
who have just addressed the house.</u>"

Verb Modifier
Adverb Phrase
Adverbial
(Adverbial and Adverbial)

_____

"<u>more highly</u> <u>than I do</u>"

Verb Modifier
Adverb Phrase
Adverbial
(Adverbial and Adverbial)

_____

"more highly"

Verb Modifier
Adverb Phrase
Adverbial
(Adverb and Adverb)

"than I do"

Adverb Modifier
Subordinate Clause
Adverbial
([Subordinate] Conjunction and Sentence)

———

"I do."

Sentence
Sentence
Sentence
([Subject] noun and [Predicate] verb)

———

of the patriotism as well as abilities
of the very worthy gentlemen
who have just addressed the house.

Adverbial Modifier
Prepositional Phrase
Adverbial

(<u>Preposition</u> and <u>Noun phrase</u>)

――――

<u>the patriotism as well as abilities</u>
<u>of the very worthy gentlemen</u>
<u>who have just addressed the house</u>.

Object of the Preposition
Noun Phrase
Nominal
(Nominal and Adjectival)

"<u>the</u> <u>patriotism</u>"

Object of the Preposition
Noun Phrase
Nominal
([<u>Limiting</u>] <u>adjective: article</u> and <u>Noun</u>

<u>as</u> <u>well as abilities of the very worthy gentlemen</u>
<u>who have just addressed the house</u>."

Noun Modifier
Prepositional Phrase
Adjectival
(<u>Preposition</u> and <u>Adverbial</u>)

――――

"<u>well</u> <u>as the abilities of the very worthy gentlemen</u>

who have just addressed the house."

(Adverb) Object of Preposition
Adverb Phrase
Adverbial
(Adverb and Adverbial)

——

"as the abilities of the very worthy gentlemen
who have just addressed the house."

Adverb Modifier
Prepositional Phrase
Adverbial
(Preposition and Nominal)

"the abilities of the very worthy gentlemen who
have just addressed the house."

Object of the Preposition
Noun Phrase
Nominal
(Nominal and Adjectival)

——

"the abilities of the very worthy gentlemen"

Object of the Preposition
Noun Phrase
Nominal

(Noun and Adjectival)

_____

"the abilities"

Object of the Preposition
Noun Phrase
Nominal
([Limiting] adjective: article and Nominal)

_____

"of the very worthy gentlemen."

Noun Modifier
Prepositional Phrase
Adjectival
(Preposition and Nominal
"the very worthy gentlemen."

Object of the Preposition
Noun Phrase
Nominal
([Limiting] adjective: article and Nominal)

_____

"very worthy gentlemen"

Object of the Preposition
Noun Phrase

Nominal
(<u>Adjectival</u> and <u>Noun</u>)

——

"<u>very worthy</u>"

Noun Modifier
Adjective Phrase
Adjectival
(<u>Adverbial</u> and <u>Adjective</u>)

——

"<u>who have just addressed the house</u>."

Noun Modifier
Relative Pronoun Clause
Adjectival
([<u>Relative</u>] <u>Pronoun</u> and <u>Verbal</u>)

"<u>have just addressed the house</u>."

Predicate
Verb Phrase
Verbal
([<u>Helping</u>] <u>verb</u> and <u>Verbal</u>)

——

"just addressed the house."

Predicate
Verb Phrase
Verbal
(Adverb and Verbal)

____

"addressed the house."

Predicate
Verb Phrase
Verbal
(Verb and [DO] Nominal)

____

"the house."

Direct Object
Noun Phrase
Nominal
([Limiting] adjective: article and Noun)

"different men often see the same subject in different lights;
and, therefore, I hope it will not be thought disrespectful to
those gentlemen if, entertaining as I do opinions of a character
very opposite to theirs, I shall speak forth my sentiments freely
and without reserve."

(Compound) Sentence
Sentence
Sentence

(<u>Sentence</u> and <u>Sentence</u>)

———

"<u>different men often see the same subject
in different lights;</u>"

Sentence
Sentence
Sentence
([<u>Subject</u>] Nominal and [<u>Predicate</u>] Verbal)

———

"<u>different men</u>"

Subject
Noun Phrase
Nominal
(<u>Adjective</u> and <u>Noun</u>)

———

"<u>often see the same subject in different lights;</u>"

Predicate
Verb Phrase
Verbal
(<u>Adverb</u> and <u>Verbal</u>)

———

"see the same subject in different lights;'

Predicate
Verb Phrase
Verbal
(Verbal and Adverbial)

————

"see the same subject"

Predicate
Verb Phrase
Verbal
(Verb and [DO] Nominal)

————

"the same subject"

Direct Object
Noun Phrase
Nominal
(Adjectival and Noun)

"the same"

Noun Modifier
Noun Phrase

Adjectival
([Limiting] adjective: article and Noun)

——

"therefore, I hope it will not be thought disrespectful to those gentlemen if, entertaining as I do opinions of a character very opposite to theirs, I shall speak forth my sentiments freely and without reserve."

Sentence
Sentence
Sentence
([Sentence modifier]: [Conjunctive] adverb and Sentence)

"I hope it will not be thought disrespectful to those gentle-men if, entertaining as I do opinions of a character very opposite to theirs, I shall speak forth my sentiments freely and without reserve."

Sentence
Sentence
Sentence
([Subject] Pronoun and [Predicate] Verbal)

——

"hope it will not be thought disrespectful to those gentle-men if, entertaining as I do opinions of a character very opposite to theirs, I shall speak forth my sentiments freely and without reserve."

Predicate
Verb Phrase
Verbal
(<u>Verb</u> and [<u>DO</u>] <u>Nominal</u>)

———

"[that] <u>it will not be thought disrespectful to those gentle-men
if, entertaining as I do opinions of a character very opposite to
theirs, I shall speak forth my sentiments freely and without
reserve</u>."

Direct Object
Subordinate Clause
Nominal
([<u>Subordinate</u>] <u>Conjunction</u> and <u>Sentence</u>)

———-

"<u>it will not be thought disrespectful to those gentle-men if,
entertaining as I do opinions of a character very opposite to
theirs, I shall speak forth my sentiments freely and without
reserve</u>."

Sentence
Sentence
Sentence
([<u>Subject</u>] <u>Pronoun</u> and [<u>Predicate</u>] <u>Verbal</u>)

———

"will not be thought disrespectful to those gentle-men if, enter-taining as I do opinions of a character very opposite to theirs, I shall speak forth my sentiments freely and without reserve."

Predicate
Verb Phrase
Verbal
([Helping] Verb and Verbal)
"not be thought disrespectful to those gentlemen if, entertaining as I do opinions of a character very opposite to theirs, I shall speak forth my sentiments freely and without reserve."

Predicate
Verb Phrase
Verbal
(Adverb and Verbal)

———

"be thought disrespectful to those gentlemen if, entertaining as I do opinions of a character very opposite to theirs, I shall speak forth my sentiments freely and without reserve."

Predicate
Verb Phrase
Verbal
([Helping] Verb and Verbal)

———

"thought disrespectful to those gentlemen if, entertaining as I do opinions of a character very opposite to theirs, I shall speak forth my sentiments freely and without reserve."

Predicate
Verb Phrase
Verbal
(Verbal and Adverbial)

_____

"thought disrespectful to those gentlemen."

Predicate
Verb Phrase
Verbal
(Verb and Adjectival)

_____

"disrespectful to those gentlemen."

Predicate Adjective
Adjective Phrase
Adjectival
(Adjective and Adverbial)

_____

"to those gentlemen."

Adjective Modifier
Prepositional Phrase

Adverbial
(<u>Preposition</u> and <u>Nominal</u>)

"<u>those</u> <u>gentlemen</u>."

Object of a Preposition
Noun Phrase
Nominal
(<u>[Limiting]</u> adjective: [demonstrative] adjective and <u>Noun</u>)

———

"<u>if, entertaining as I do opinions of a character very opposite to</u>
<u>theirs, I shall speak forth my sentiments freely and without</u>
<u>reserve</u>."

Verb Modifier
Subordinate Clause
Adverbial
(<u>[Subordinate] conjunction</u> and <u>Sentence</u>)

———

"<u>entertaining as I do opinions of a character very opposite to</u>
<u>theirs, I shall speak forth my sentiments freely and without</u>
<u>reserve</u>."

Sentence
Sentence

Sentence
([Sentence modifier] Verbal and Sentence)

———-

"entertaining as I do opinions of a character very opposite to theirs,"

Sentence Modifier
Verb Phrase
Verbal
(Verbal and [DO]Nominal)

———

"entertaining as I do"

Sentence Modifier
Verb Phrase
Verbal
(Verbal and Adverbial)
"as I do"

Verb Modifier
Subordinate Clause
Adverbial
([Subordinate] Conjunction and Sentence)

———

"I do"

Sentence
Sentence
Sentence
([Subject] Pronoun and [Predicate] Verb)

——

"opinions of a character very opposite to theirs,"

Direct Object
Noun Phrase
Nominal
(Noun and Adjectival)

——

"of a character very opposite to theirs,"

Noun Modifier
Prepositional Phrase
Adjectival
(Preposition and Nominal)

——

"a character very opposite to theirs,"

Object of a Preposition
Noun Phrase

Nominal
(<u>Nominal</u> and <u>Adjectival</u>)

———

"<u>a</u> <u>character</u>"

Object of a Preposition
Noun Phrase
Nominal
([<u>Limiting</u>] Adjective: indefinite article and <u>Noun</u>)

"<u>very opposite</u> <u>to theirs,</u>"

Noun Modifier
Adjective Phrase
Adjectival
(<u>Adjectival</u> and <u>Adverbial</u>)

———

"<u>very</u> <u>opposite</u>"

Noun Modifier
Adjective Phrase
Adjectival
(<u>Adverbial</u> and <u>Adjectival</u>)

———

"<u>to</u> <u>theirs,</u>"

Adjective Modifier
Prepositional Phrase
Adverbial
(<u>Preposition</u> and <u>Pronoun</u>)

———

"<u>I</u> <u>shall speak forth my sentiments freely and without reserve</u>."

Sentence
Sentence
Sentence
([Subject] Pronoun and [Predicate] Verbal)

"<u>shall</u> <u>speak forth my sentiments freely and without reserve</u>."

Predicate
Verb Phrase
Verbal
([<u>Helping</u>] <u>verb</u> and <u>Verbal</u>)

———

"<u>speak forth my sentiments</u> <u>freely and without reserve</u>."

Predicate
Verb Phrase
Verbal
(<u>Verbal</u> and <u>Adverbial</u>)

———

"speak forth my sentiments"

Predicate
Verb Phrase
Verbal
(Verbal and [DO] Nominal)

———

"speak forth"

Predicate
Verb Phrase
Verbal
(Verb and Adverb)

"my sentiments"

Direct Object
Noun Phrase
Nominal
([Limiting] adjective: [possessive] adjective and Noun)

———

"freely and without reserve."

Verb Modifier
Adverb Phrase

(Compound) Adverbial
(<u>Adverb</u> and <u>Adverbial</u>)

——

"<u>without</u> <u>reserve</u>."

Verb Modifier
Prepositional Phrase
Adverbial

(<u>Preposition</u> and <u>Noun</u>)

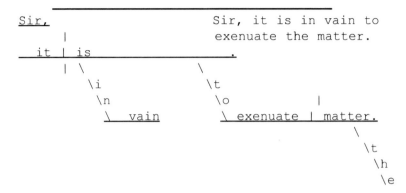

```
<u>Sir,</u>                                    Sir, it is in vain to
         |                           exenuate the matter.
    <u>it  |  is                        .</u>
        |  \                  \
          \i               \t
           \n               \o              |
            \   vain         \ exenuate  | <u>matter.</u>
                                             \
                                              \t
                                               \h
                                                \e
```

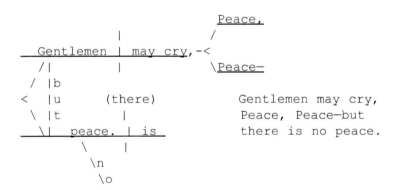

```
                              <u>Peace,</u>
                  |          /
      <u>Gentlemen  |  may cry,</u> -<
       /|          |         \<u>Peace—</u>
      / |b
    <  |u      (there)        Gentlemen may cry,
     \ |t         |           Peace, Peace—but
      \| <u>peace. | is</u>          there is no peace.
          \    |
           \n
            \o
```

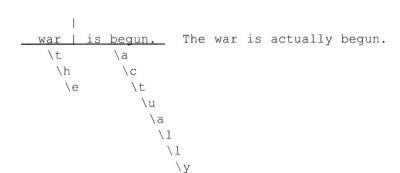

```
        |
    <u>war | is begun.</u>   The war is actually begun.
      \t       \a
       \h       \c
        \e       \t
                  \u
                   \a
                    \l
                     \l
                      \y
```

```
    gale     | will bring | clash
 \     \    _  | \           \     \
  \T   \n  _     \t          \t   \o
   \h   \e  _     \o          \h   \f
    \e   \x  _     \ ears      \e   \  arms.
       \t  _        \             \
          _          \o              \r
           _          \u              \e
            _          \r              \s
             |                          \o
         that | sweeps                   \u
           |   \                          \n
               \t                          \d
```

```
           |
brethren | are   .                Our brethren are
  \       | \    \                already in the field.
   \O      \a  \i
    \u      \l  \n
     \r      \r  \  field.
             \e    \
              \a    \t
               \d    \h
                \y    \e
```

```
       |        \              Why stand we here idle?
    We | stand  \ idle?
       |  \      \
         \h      \W
          \e      \h
           \r      \y
            \e
```

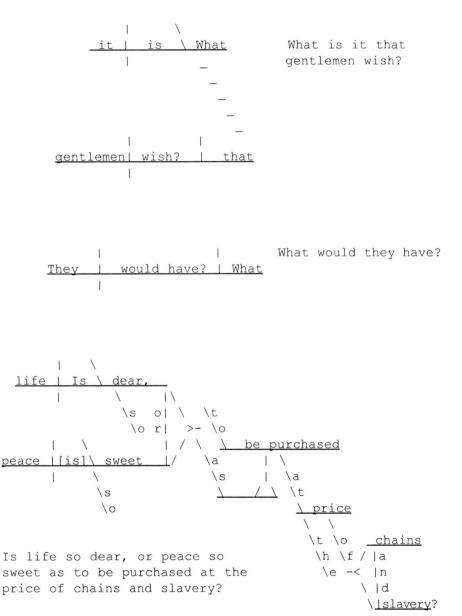

What is it that
gentlemen wish?

What would they have?

Is life so dear, or peace so
sweet as to be purchased at the
price of chains and slavery?

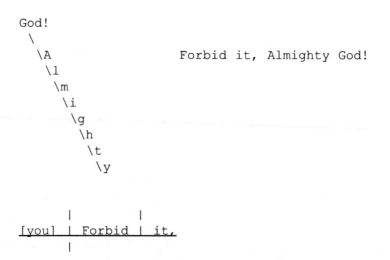

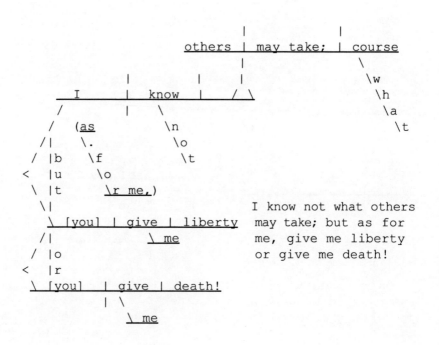

John F. Kennedy, Inaugural Address. Friday, January 20, 1961

Heavy snow fell the night before the inauguration, but thoughts about canceling the plans were overruled. The election of 1960 had been close, and the Democratic Senator from Massachusetts was eager to gather support for his agenda. He attended Holy Trinity Catholic Church in Georgetown that morning before joining President Eisenhower to travel to the Capitol. The Congress had extended the East Front, and the inaugural platform spanned the new addition. The oath of office was administered by Chief Justice Earl Warren. Robert Frost read one of his poems at the ceremony. Mr. Kennedy's speech follows:

"Vice President Johnson, Mr. Speaker, Mr. Chief Justice, President Eisenhower, Vice President Nixon, President Truman, reverend clergy, fellow citizens, we observe today not a victory of party, but a celebration of freedom—symbolizing an end, as well as a beginning—signifying renewal, as well as change. For I have sworn before you and Almighty God the same solemn oath our forebears prescribed nearly a century and three-quarters ago.

The world is very different now. For man holds in his mortal hands the power to abolish all forms of human poverty and all forms of human life. And yet the same revolutionary beliefs for which our forebears fought are still at issue around the globe—the belief that the rights of man come not from the generosity of the state, but from the hand of God.

We dare not forget today that we are the heirs of that first revolution. Let the word go forth from this time and place, to friend and foe alike, that the torch has been passed to a new generation of Americans—born in this century, tempered by war, disciplined by a hard and bitter peace, proud of our ancient heritage—and unwilling to witness or permit the slow undoing of those human rights to which this Nation has always been committed, and to which we are committed today at home and around the world.

Let every nation know, whether it wishes us well or ill, that we shall pay any price, bear any burden, meet any hardship, support any friend, oppose any foe, in order to assure the survival and the success of liberty.

This much we pledge—and more.

To those old allies whose cultural and spiritual origins we share, we pledge the loyalty of faithful friends. United, there is little we cannot do in a host of cooperative ventures. Divided, there is little we can do—for we dare not meet a powerful challenge at odds and split asunder.

To those new States whom we welcome to the ranks of the free, we pledge our word that one form of colonial control shall not have passed away merely to be replaced by a far more iron tyranny. We shall not always expect to find them supporting our view. But we shall always hope to find them strongly supporting their own freedom—and to remember that, in the past, those who foolishly sought power by riding the back of the tiger ended up inside.

To those peoples in the huts and villages across the globe struggling to break the bonds of mass misery, we pledge our best efforts to help them help themselves, for whatever period is required—not because the Communists may be doing it, not because we seek their votes, but because it is right. If a free society cannot help the many who are poor, it cannot save the few who are rich.

To our sister republics south of our border, we offer a special pledge—to convert our good words into good deeds—in a new alliance for progress—to assist free men and free governments in casting off the chains of poverty. But this peaceful revolution of hope cannot become the prey of hostile powers. Let all our neighbors know that we shall join with them to oppose aggression or subversion anywhere in the

Americas. And let every other power know that this Hemisphere intends to remain the master of its own house.

To that world assembly of sovereign states, the United Nations, our last best hope in an age where the instruments of war have far outpaced the instruments of peace, we renew our pledge of support—to prevent it from becoming merely a forum for invective—to strengthen its shield of the new and the weak—and to enlarge the area in which its writ may run.

Finally, to those nations who would make themselves our adversary, we offer not a pledge but a request: that both sides begin anew the quest for peace, before the dark powers of destruction unleashed by science engulf all humanity in planned or accidental self-destruction.

We dare not tempt them with weakness. For only when our arms are sufficient beyond doubt can we be certain beyond doubt that they will never be employed.

But neither can two great and powerful groups of nations take comfort from our present course—both sides overburdened by the cost of modern weapons, both rightly alarmed by the steady spread of the deadly atom, yet both racing to alter that uncertain balance of terror that stays the hand of mankind's final war.

So let us begin anew—remembering on both sides that civility is not a sign of weakness, and sincerity is always subject to proof. Let us never negotiate out of fear. But let us never fear to negotiate.

Let both sides explore what problems unite us instead of belaboring those problems which divide us.

Let both sides, for the first time, formulate serious and precise proposals for the inspection and control of arms—and bring the absolute power to destroy other nations under the absolute control of all nations.

Let both sides seek to invoke the wonders of science instead of its terrors. Together let us explore the stars, conquer the deserts, eradicate disease, tap the ocean depths, and encourage the arts and commerce.

Let both sides unite to heed in all corners of the earth the command of Isaiah—to "undo the heavy burdens...and to let the oppressed go free."

And if a beachhead of cooperation may push back the jungle of suspicion, let both sides join in creating a new endeavor, not a new balance of power, but a new world of law, where the strong are just and the weak secure and the peace preserved.

All this will not be finished in the first 100 days. Nor will it be finished in the first 1,000 days, nor in the life of this Administration, nor even perhaps in our lifetime on this planet. But let us begin.

In your hands, my fellow citizens, more than in mine, will rest the final success or failure of our course. Since this country was founded, each generation of Americans has been summoned to give testimony to its national loyalty. The graves of young Americans who answered the call to service surround the globe.

Now the trumpet summons us again—not as a call to bear arms, though arms we need; not as a call to battle, though embattled we are— but a call to bear the burden of a long twilight struggle, year in and year out, "rejoicing in hope, patient in tribulation"—a struggle against the common enemies of man: tyranny, poverty, disease, and war itself.

Can we forge against these enemies a grand and global alliance, North and South, East and West, that can assure a more fruitful life for all mankind? Will you join in that historic effort?

In the long history of the world, only a few generations have been granted the role of defending freedom in its hour of maximum danger. I do not shrink from this responsibility—I welcome it. I do not believe that any of us would exchange places with any other people or any other generation. The energy, the faith, the devotion which we bring to this endeavor will light our country and all who serve it—and the glow from that fire can truly light the world.

And so, my fellow Americans: ask not what your country can do for you—ask what you can do for your country.

My fellow citizens of the world: ask not what America will do for you, but what together we can do for the freedom of man.

Finally, whether you are citizens of America or citizens of the world, ask of us the same high standards of strength and sacrifice which we ask of you. With a good conscience our only sure reward, with history the final judge of our deeds, let us go forth to lead the land we love, asking His blessing and His help, but knowing that here on earth God's work must truly be our own.

The University of Oklahoma Law Center © 2000 Bartleby.com

From The Irish Press of Friday June 4th, 1976…
Chief Seattle's Speech
In 1854, "The Great White Chief" in Washington made an offer for a large area of Indian land and promised a "reservation" for the Indian people. Chief Seattle's reply, published here in full, to mark World Environment Day tomorrow, has been described as one of the most beautiful and profound statements on the environment ever made:

How can you buy or sell the sky, the warmth of the land? The idea is strange to us. If we do not own the freshness of the air and the sparkle of the water, how can you buy them? Every part of the Earth is sacred to my people. Every shining pine needle, every sandy shore, every mist in the dark woods, every clear and humming insect is holy in the memory and experience of my people. The sap which courses through the trees carries the memory and experience of my people. The sap which courses through the trees carries the memories of the red man.

The white man's dead forget the country of their birth when they go to walk among the stars. Our dead never forget this beautiful Earth, for it is the mother of the red man. We are part of the Earth and it is part of us. The perfumed flowers are our sisters, the deer, the horse, the great eagle, these are our brothers. The rocky crests, the juices in the meadows, the body heat of the pony, and the man, all belong to the same family.

So, when the Great Chief in Washington sends word that he wishes to buy our land, he asks much of us. The Great White Chief sends word he will reserve us a place so that we can live comfortably to ourselves. He will be our father and we will be his children. So we will consider your offer to buy land. But it will not be easy. For this land is sacred to us.

This shining water that moves in streams and rivers is not just water but the blood of our ancestors. If we sell you land, you must remember that it is sacred blood of our ancestors. If we sell you land, you must remember that it is sacred, and you must teach your children that it is sacred and that each ghostly reflection in the clear water of the lakes tells of events in the life of my people. The waters murmur is the voice of my father's father.

The rivers of our brothers they quench our thirst. The rivers carry our canoes and feed our children. If we sell you our land, you must remember to teach your children that the rivers are our brothers, and yours, and you must henceforth give the rivers the kindness that you would give my brother. We know that the white man does not understand our ways. One portion of land is the same to him as the next, for he is a stranger who comes in the night and takes from the land whatever he needs. The Earth is not his brother, but his enemy and when he has conquered it, he moves on. He leaves his father's graves behind, and he does not care. He kidnaps the Earth from his children, and he does not care.

BIRTHRIGHT

His father's grave, and his children's birthright are forgotten. He treats his mother, the Earth, and his brother, the same, as things to be bought, plundered, sold like sheep or bright beads. His appetite will devour the Earth and leave behind only a desert.

I do not know. Our ways are different from yours ways. The sight of your cities pains the eyes of the red man. But perhaps it is because the red man is a savage and does not understand.

PRECIOUS

The air is precious to the red man, for all things share the same breath—the beast, the tree, the man, they all share the same breath. The white man does not seem to notice the air he breathes. Like a man dying for many days, he is numb to the stench. But if we sell you our land, you must remember that the air is precious to us, that the air shares its spirit with all the life it supports. The wind that gave our grandfather his first breath also receives his last sigh. And if we sell you our land, you must keep it apart and sacred, as a place where even the white man can go to taste the wind that is sweetened by the meadow's flowers.

So we will consider your offer to buy our land. If we decide to accept, I will make one condition—the white man must treat the beasts of this land as his brothers.

I am a savage and do not understand any other way. I have seen a thousand rotting buffaloes on the prairie, left by the white man who shot them from a passing train. I am a savage and do not understand how the smoking iron horse can be made more important than the buffalo that we kill only to stay alive.

What is man without the beasts? If all the beasts were gone, man would die from a great loneliness of the spirit. For whatever happens to the beasts, soon happens to man. All things are connected.

RESPECT

You must teach your children that the ground beneath their feet is the ashes of our grandfathers. So that they will respect the land, tell your children that the Earth is rich with the lives of our kin. Teach your children what we have taught our children, that the Earth is our mother. Whatever befalls the Earth befalls the sons of the Earth. If men spit upon the ground, they spit upon themselves.

This we know—the Earth does not belong to man—man belongs to the Earth. This we know. All things are connected like the blood which unites one family. All things are connected.

Whatever befalls the Earth—befalls the sons of the Earth. Man did not weave the web of life—he is merely a strand in it. Whatever he does to the web, he does to himself.

Even the white man, whose God walks and talks with him as friend to friend, cannot be exempt from the common destiny. We may be brothers after all. We shall see. One thing we know, which the white man may one day discover—Our God is the same God. You may think now that you own Him as you wish to own our land, but you cannot. He is the God of man, and His compassion is equal for red man and the white. The Earth is precious to Him, and to harm the Earth is to heap contempt on its creator. The whites too shall pass, perhaps sooner than all other tribes.

But in your perishing you will shine brightly, fired by the strength of the God who brought you to this land and for some special purpose gave you dominion over this land and over the red man. That destiny is a mystery to us, for we do not understand when the buffalo are slaughtered, the wild horses tamed, the secret corners of the forest heavy with scent of many men, and the view of the ripe hills blotted by talking wires. Where is the thicket? Gone. Where is the Eagle? Gone. The end of living and the beginning of survival.

End of Extract from The Irish Press of Friday June 4th, 1976.

NELSON MANDELA'S ADDRESS ON HIS RELEASE FROM PRISON

'We have waited too long for our freedom…' The full text of Nelson Mandela's address to the people on the day of his unconditional release after twenty-seven years in prison. Grand Parade, Cape Town—11th February, 1990 ————————————

Friends, Comrades and Fellow South Africans, I greet you in the name of peace, democracy and freedom for all. I stand here before you, not as a prophet, but as a humble servant of you, the people. Your tireless and heroic sacrifices have made it possible for me to be here today. I therefore place the remaining years of my life in your hands. On this day of my release I extend my sincere and warmest gratitude to the millions of my compatriots and those in every corner of the globe who have campaigned tirelessly for my release. I extend special greetings to the people of Cape Town, the city which has been my home for three decades. Your mass marches and other forms of struggle have served as a constant source of strength to all political prisoners. I salute the African National Congress. It has fulfilled our every expectation in its role as leader of the great march to freedom. I salute our President, Comrade Oliver Tambo, for leading the ANC even under the most difficult circumstances. I salute the rank and file members of the ANC. You have sacrificed life and limb in the pursuit of the noble cause of our struggle. I salute combatants of Umkhonto we Sizwe, like Solomon Mahlangu and Ashley Kriel, who have paid the ultimate price for the freedom of all South Africans. I salute the South African Communist Party for its sterling contribution to the struggle for democracy. You have survived 40 years of unrelenting persecution. The memory of great communists like Moses Kotane, Yusuf Dadoo, Bram Fischer and Moses Mabhida will be cherished for generations to come. I salute General Secretary Joe Slovo—one of our finest patriots.

We are heartened by the fact that the alliance between ourselves and the Party remains as strong as it always was. I salute the United Democratic Front, Cosatu, the National Education Crisis Committee, the South African Youth Congress, the Transvaal and Natal Indian Congresses and the many other formations of the Mass Democratic Movement. Conscience of Whites I also salute the Black Sash and the National Union of South African Students. We note with pride that you have acted as the conscience of white South Africans. Even during the darkest days in the history of your struggle you held the flag of liberty high. The large-scale mass mobilisation of the past few years is one of the key factors which led to the opening of the final chapter of our struggle. I extend my greetings to the working class of our country. Your organised strength is the pride of our movement. You remain the most dependable force in the struggle to end exploitation and oppression. I pay tribute to the many religious communities who carried the campaign for justice forward when the organisations of our people were silenced. I greet the traditional leaders of our country. Many among you continue to walk in the footsteps of great heroes like Hintsa and Sekhukhuni. I pay tribute to the endless heroism of the youth. You, the young lions, have energised our entire struggle. I pay tribute to the mothers and wives and sisters of our nation. You are the rock-hard foundation of our struggle. Apartheid has inflicted more pain on you than on anyone else. Frontline Sacrifices On this occasion we thank the world community for their great contribution to the anti-apartheid struggle. Without your support our struggle would not have reached this advanced stage. The sacrifices of the Frontline States will be remembered by South Africans forever. My salutations will be incomplete without expressing my deep appreciation for the strength given to me during my long and lonely years in prison by my beloved wife and family. I am convinced that your pain and suffering was far greater than my own. Before I go any further, I wish to make the point that I intend making only a few preliminary comments at this stage. I will make a more public statement only after I have had the opportunity to consult with my comrades. Today the majority of South Africans, black and white, recognise that apartheid has no future. It has to be ended by our own decisive mass action in order to build peace and security. The mass campaign of defiance and other actions of our organisation and people can only culminate with the establishment of democracy. The apartheid destruction on our sub-continent is incalculable. The fabric of family life of millions of our people has been shattered. Millions are homeless and unemployed, our economy lies in ruins and our people are embroiled in political strife. Armed Struggle—No Option but to Continue Our resort to the armed struggle in 1960, with the formation of the military wing of the ANC, Umkhonto we Sizwe, was a purely defensive action against the violence of apartheid. The factors which necessitated the armed struggle still exist today. We have no option but to continue. We express the hope that a climate conducive to a negotiated settlement will be created soon so that there may no longer be the need for the armed struggle. I am a loyal and disciplined member of the African National Congress. I am therefore in full agreement with all of its objectives, strategies and tactics. The need to unite the people of our country is as important a task now as it always has been. No individual leader is able to take on this enormous task on his own. It is our task as leaders to place our views before our organization and to allow the democratic structures to decide on the way forward. On the question of democratic practice, I feel duty-bound to make the point that a leader of the movement is a person who has been democratically elected at a national conference. This is a principle which must be upheld without any exceptions. Insistence on a Meeting Today I wish to report to you that my talks with the government have been aimed at normalising the political situation in the country. We have not as yet begun discussing the basic demands of the struggle. I wish to stress that I, myself, have at no time entered into negotiation about the future of our country, except to insist on a meeting between the ANC and the government. Mr. De Klerk has gone further than any other Nationalist president in taking real steps to normalise the situation. However, there are further steps as outlined in the Harare Declaration that have to be met before negotiations on the basic demands of our people can begin. I reiterate our call for, inter alia, the immediate ending of the State of Emergency and the freeing of all, and not only some, political prisoners. Only such a normalised situation which allows for free political activity, can allow us to consult our people in order to obtain a mandate. Not Behind the Backs of the People The people need to be consulted on who will negotiate and on the content of such negotiations. Negotiations cannot take place above the heads or behind the backs of our people. It is our belief that the future of our country can only be determined by a body which is democratically elected on a non-racial basis. Negotiations on the dismantling of apartheid will have to address the overwhelming demands of our people for a democratic, non-racial and unitary South Africa. There must be an end to white monopoly on political power and a fundamental restructuring of our political and economic system to ensure that the inequalities of apartheid are addressed and our society thoroughly democratised. It must be added that Mr De Klerk himself is a man of integrity who is acutely aware of the danger of a public figure not honoring his undertakings. But as an organisation we base our policy and strategies on the harsh reality we are faced with and this reality is that we are still suffering under the policy of the Nationalist government. Our struggle has reached a decisive moment. We call on our people to seize this moment so that the process towards democracy is rapid and uninterrupted. We have waited too long for our freedom. We can no longer wait. Now is the time to intensify the struggle on all fronts. To relax our effort now would be a mistake which generations to come will not be able to forgive. The Sight of Freedom The sight of freedom looming on the horizon should encourage us to redouble our efforts. It is only through disciplined mass action that our victory can be assured. We call on our white compatriots to join us in the shaping of a new South Africa. The freedom movement is a political home for you too. We call on the international community to continue the campaign to isolate the apartheid regime. To lift sanctions now would be to run the risk of aborting the process towards the complete eradication of apartheid. Our march to freedom is irreversible. We must not allow fear to stand in our way. Universal suffrage on a common voters' roll in a united, democratic and non-racial South Africa is the only way to peace and racial harmony. In conclusion, I wish to quote my own words during my trial in 1964. They are as true today as they were then. I quote: I have fought against white domination and I have fought against black domination. I have carried the ideal of a democratic and free society in which all persons live together in harmony and with equal opportunity. It is an ideal which I hope to live for and to achieve. But, if needs be, it is an ideal for which I am prepared to die. I hope you will disperse with dignity and not a single one of you should do anything which will make other people say that we can't control our own people.

FOR FURTHER INFORMATION CONTACT: ANC, PO BOX 31791, LUSAKA, ZAMBIA OR ANC, PO BOX 38, LONDON N1 9PR, UNITED KINGDOM .

Ain't I A Woman?
by Sojourner Truth
Delivered 1851 at the Women's Convention in Akron, Ohio

Well, children, where there is so much racket there must be something out of kilter. I think that 'twixt the Negroes of the South and the women at the North, all talking about rights, the white men will be in a fix pretty soon. But what's all this here talking about?

That man over there says that women need to be helped into carriages, and lifted over ditches, and to have the best place everywhere. Nobody ever helps me into carriages, or over mud-puddles, or gives me any best place! And ain't I a woman? Look at me! Look at my arm! I have ploughed and planted, and gathered into barns, and no man could head me! And ain't I a woman? I could work as much and eat as much as a man—when I could get it—and bear the lash as well! And ain't I a woman? I have borne thirteen children, and seen most all sold off to slavery, and when I cried out with my mother's grief, none but Jesus heard me!

And ain't I a woman?

Then they talk about this thing in the head; what's this they call it? [member of audience whispers, "intellect"] That's it, honey. What's that got to do with women's rights or Negroes' rights? If my cup won't hold but a pint, and yours holds a quart, wouldn't you be mean not to let me have my little half measure full?

Then that little man in black there, he says women can't have as much rights as men, 'cause Christ wasn't a woman! Where did your Christ come from? Where did your Christ come from? From God and a woman! Man had nothing to do with Him.

If the first woman God ever made was strong enough to turn the world upside down all alone, these women together ought to be able to turn it back , and get it right side up again! And now they is asking to do it, the men better let them.

Obliged to you for hearing me, and now old Sojourner ain't got nothing more to say.

About the Author

Dr. Susan M. Leist is an Associate Professor of English and Humanities at the State University of New York's College at Buffalo. She welcomes e-mail communication at "sleist@bscmail.buffalostate.edu".

Dr. Melvin J. Hoffman is a Professor of English at the State University of New York's College at Buffalo.

Notes

1   **Reed-Kellog, 1909.**

2   **Campbell, Website.**

3   **Kolln, 1981.**

4   **Hartwell, 1985.**

5   **Francis, 1954.**

6   **Kolln, 1981: 140**

7   **Assembly for Teaching Grammar, Website**

8   **Del Prince, 1998.**

Bibliography

<u>Books:</u>

Jespersen, Jens Otto Harry. 1933. Essentials of English Gram-mar. New York: Henry Holt.

[This is a classic Historical-Linguistic view of English grammar.]

_____. 1962. Growth and Structure of the English Language. 9th.Ed. Oxford: Basil Blackwell. (Original Edition: 1938.)

[Jespersen tries to widen the audience for the History of English.]

Kolln, Martha. 1998. Rhetorical Grammar: Grammatical Choices, Rhetorical Effects. 3rd. edition. Boston: Allyn & Bacon.

[This applies grammar to teaching Rhetoric, mixing transformational and traditional terminology.]

Kolln, Martha. 1997. Understanding English Grammar. Robert Funk. (Contributor) 5th. edition. Boston: Allyn & Bacon.

[This textbook mixes traditional, structural and transformational grammar-with mostly traditional diagrams.]

Lester, Mark. 1990. Grammar in the Classroom. NY: MacMillan Publishing Company.

[Lester eclectically mixes traditional, structural and transforma-tional grammar-with mostly traditional diagrams, and appendices on class-room applications and the history of grammar.]

Quirk, Randolph; Greenbaum, Sidney; Leech, Geoffrey; and Svartik. (Jan. 1985). A Comprehensive Grammar of the English Language. London: Longman. .

[This very comprehensive grammar of the English Language is mostly, but not entirely, tranformationally oriented]

Reed, Alonzo & Kellog, Brainerd. 19O9. Higher Lessons in English. Rev. NY: C. E. Merril Co. (Rev. of prior rev.: NY: Clark & Maynard,1885.)

[Traditional diagrams come from this mother of U.S. DIAGRAMING.]

Shaughnessy, Mina. 1977. Errors and Expectations: A Guide for the Teacher of Basic Writing. New York: Oxford University Press.

[This is an important book on grammar and composition for teachers.]

Weaver, Constance. 1996.Teaching Grammar in Context. Ports-mouth, NH: Boynton/Cook.

[Weaver draws on research to suggest when, how and why grammar should be taught to enhance teaching writing.]

Articles:

Dykema, Karl W. 1961. "Where our Grammar Came from." College English. 22: 455-65.

[This briefly traces grammar study from Classical to Medieval times, with four grammar definitions. See Francis and Hartwell.]

Farren, Sean. 1992. "Knowledge about Language: An Old Controversy in New Programmes." Language Culture & Curriculum. 5.3: 185-197.*

[Debate on knowledge of language (KAL) in British and Northern Irish English teaching moves from the 1975 Bullock Report, which ended grammar teaching, to the present.]

Francis, W. Nelson. 1954. "Revolution in Grammar." Quarterly Journal of Speech. 4O: 299-312.

[Francis distinguishes three meanings of the term, grammar. Compare Dykema and Hartwell.]

Glau, Gregory R. 1993. "Mirroring Ourselves? The Pedagogy of Early Grammar Texts." Rhetoric Review. 11.2: 418-435.*

[Glau argues little change in grammar-text use in over 2OO years, reviews early grammar texts' origins and use, alleging that gram-mar text uses mirror instructors' perceptions of their students.]

Hartung, Charles V. 1962. "The Persistence of Tradition in Grammar." Quarterly Journal of Speech. 48:174-186.

[This briefly outlines the history of grammar study and controversies from the Classical Greek to Structuralist periods.]

Hartwell, Patrick. 1985. "Grammar, Grammars and the Teaching of Grammar." College English. 47:1O5-1O7.

[This oft-cited review of major controversies in grammar teaching explores the role of ambiguity in the term grammar itself and provides five distinct definitions. See Dykema and Francis.]

Kenyon, John S. 1948. "Cultural Levels and Functional Varieties of English." College English. 1O: 31-36.

[Kenyon distinguishes situation-based choices of linguistic variants e.g. public and private uses from social dialect differences.]

Kolln, Martha. 1981. "Closing the Books on Alchemy." CCC. 32: 139-151.

[Kolln faults studies against grammar in teaching writing. She supports acknowledging and using grammar to teach writing.]

McMillan, James B. 1954. "Summary of Nineteenth Century Historical and Comparative Linguistics." College Composition and Communication. 5: 14O-149.

[The author claims that 19th. Century failure to clearly distinguish Philology, Linguistics and Rhetoric still caused problems.]

Renwick, Mitzi K. 1994. "Real Research into the Real Problems of Grammar and Usage Instruction." English Journal. 83.6: 29-32.

[This English teacher studies her students' language patterns using them to adjust her teaching and noting the difficulty in altering habits of non-standard usage in speech and writing.]

Simmons, Eileen A. 1991. "Ain't we Never Gonna Study No Grammar?" English Journal. 8O: 8:48-51.

[This describes dilemmas from teaching Standard American En-gilt while accepting and not judging nonstandard dialects. The teacher uses "Pygmalion" by George Bernard Shaw to show students why they need to learn SAE.]

Tomlinson, David. 1994. "Errors in the Research into Effective Grammar Teaching." English in Education. 28.1: 2O-26.*

[The author questions whether sustained instruction in "basics" is wrongly ignored, challenges teachers who claim that grammar instruction is unneeded, and negatively reviews two research studies supposedly proving grammar teaching's ineffectiveness.]

Vavra, Ed. 1993. "Welcome to the Shoe Store?" English Journal. 82.5: 81-84.

[Vavra describes discussions of grammar teaching by English teachers. He asserts several effective ways to teach grammar.]

Warner, Ann L. 1993. "If the Shoe No Longer Fits, Wear it Anyway?" English Journal. 82.5: 76-8O.

[Warner presents facts gathered informally from junior high English teachers about teaching grammar, includes disagreements on the feasibility of teaching grammar in English classrooms, reasons for grammar teaching, and methods for teaching it.]

Websites:

Rhetoric Website Page Listing George Campbell's Contributions. *http://bradley.bradley.edu/~ell/campbell.html*

[…Standards…are…reputable, national, and present.]

Charles Darling. GUIDE TO GRAMMAR AND WRITING. *http://webster.commnet.edu/HP/pages/darling/original.htm*
[The work steers between technical and traditional terminology.]
The NCTE Assembly for the Teaching of English Grammar.

http://www2.pct.edu/courses/evavra/ATEG/
[This web page is devoted to title subject.]

Dr. Johanna Rubba. Syntax: Terms and Concepts.
http://www.multimedia.calpoly.edu/libarts/jrubba/SyntaxT&C.html
[This work has technical (government binding) but mostly traditional terminology.]

Dr. Ed Vavra. KISS Grammar Course.
http://www2.pct.edu/courses/evavra/ED498/SP/index.htm
[Vavra provides a curriculum from 7th. through the 11th. grades.]

Student Essay:

Del Prince, Nicole. 1998. "Report on Interviews with Secondary Education Teachers on What They Thought and Taught about Grammar." October 4.

Index

135